The Twelve Steps as a Path to Enlightenment

How the Buddha Works the Steps

Dorena Rode

Printed in the United States of America

A.A.'s Twelve Steps and brief excerpts from Alcoholics Anonymous are reprinted with permission of Alcoholics Anonymous World Services, Inc. ("AAWS"). Permission to reprint these excerpts does not mean that AAWS has reviewed or approved the contents of this publication, or that AAWS necessarily agrees with the views expressed herein. A.A. is a program of recovery from alcoholism only – use of these excerpts in connection with programs and activities which are patterned after A.A., but which address other problems, or in any other non A.A. context, does not imply otherwise.

The Mandala of the Steps to Enlightenment by Je Tsongkapa (chapter 3) and the karmic consequences (chapter 5) are reprinted from the Asian Classics Institute's course materials (ACIdharma.org). The majority of the Tibetan Buddhist thought included in this book is inspired by the Asian Classics Institute's coursework developed and taught by Geshe Michel Roach. This material is used with permission. The Asian Classics Institute has not reviewed this work.

Rode, Dorena, 1964-
The twelve steps as a path to enlightenment: how the Buddha works the steps/Dorena Rode

ISBN: 1941894046
ISBN-13: 978-1-941894-04-0

1. Twelve Step programs–Religious aspects–Buddhism. 2. Religious life–Buddhism. 3. Self-help techniques–Religious aspects–Buddhism. 4. Compulsive Behavior–Moral and ethical aspects. 5. Wisdom–Religious aspects–Buddhism. 6. Spiritual life–Buddhism.

TESLI

The Enlightenment & Simple Living Institute
TESLI.org

PLEDGE TO COMPOSE THE WORK

Many people struggle with the concept of a higher power or God in the meeting rooms of Twelve Step programs. This seems to impede their ability to embrace a spiritual program that can lead to greater happiness and ultimately to freedom from all suffering. I am one of those that has been unable to accept the concept of a higher power, despite over twenty years in the program. I have been tempted many times to leave the fellowship. Yet, despite having this inability to believe in God, I have found that the program works fine without the belief in a higher power. Indeed, there are a lot of "lower" powers that have been able to help me become happier and more peaceful with each year.

Recently, I completed intensive course work examining the Asian classics which form the foundation of Buddhism. (See Asian Classics Institute in the resource section at the end of this book.) What I learned was very helpful in explaining how the Steps work. Indeed, they work fine without a higher power, just differently from the way the original authors imagined.

In this presentation I undertake an interpretation of the spiritual principles embodied in the Steps from a Buddhist perspective. There are a number of different schools of thought and religious orders that derive their tenets from the Buddha's teachings. This work is specifically based on Tibetan Buddhism of the Gelug School. (The school in which the lineage of the Dalai Lamas belongs.)

My intention in composing this work is to deepen my integration of the spiritual principles that make up the path to enlightenment. My hope is that others might also benefit from this writing and that together, as we "trudge the road of happy destiny", we may know greater peace that will spread to all others. In addition, I pray this work will help me remember to practice the Twelve Steps in all areas of my life at all times.

ACKNOWLEDGEMENTS

I give thanks to the source of all my good and the many guides and teachers that support and bless me. This work is based on the teachings of Geshe Michael Roach and I am happy to be able to share the world view I learned from him. In addition, without the many anonymous people that have created and continued the Twelve Step fellowships worldwide, this work would not exist, nor would my life be as rich and wonderful as it is. Finally, although I have enjoyed writing this tremendously, I must admit that I do not think I would have finished it, if MaryJo had not requested it.

CONTENTS

INTRODUCTION

Background

Twenty years of Twelve Step recovery made me "happy, joyous, and free" – but not all the time. I came into Twelve Step programs expecting to learn how to be happy <u>all</u> the time and instead I was told that the best I could expect was to be able to gracefully accept life on life's terms. The message of the program was that I did not have to suffer over my suffering, but that idea of eternal bliss was just a fantasy.

The Big Book of Alcoholics Anonymous tells us that more will be revealed, and this is certainly true. I have since learned that the Buddha taught how to <u>permanently</u> end all suffering. This is exactly what I want! The spiritual journey does not end with acceptance but continues until we reach a complete cessation of all unpleasantness. This is the message and vision I want to give back to the fellowships of Twelve Step programs.

Overview

The Twelve Steps as a Path to Enlightenment - How the Buddha Works the Steps examines the Twelve Steps and explains how they parallel the steps the Buddha outlined for reaching ultimate enlightenment. This treatise takes the bold move of integrating the Buddhist's path to enlightenment with the Twelve Step program, resulting in a complete spiritual path that can be used to relieve addictive and compulsive behavior as well as more subtle forms of suffering.

First and foremost, this is a book on how to end suffering that combines two methods that people generally accept as useful: The Twelve Steps and Buddha's teachings. It is not about adding some Buddhism to the Twelve Steps; it is about taking Buddhism and reframing it in the Twelve Step model. This book fills the following gaps:

- Gives Buddhists an alternate Twelve Step guide and text.

- Integrates the Twelve Steps with the Buddhist's path to enlightenment.

- Introduces a new world view to spiritual seekers that believe there is no God.

- Provides westerners with a clear guide for spiritual progression and a complete method for reaching enlightenment based on ancient Buddhists texts, but in a modern format.

A Twelve Step Guide for the Buddhist.

About six million people in the United States are Buddhist. The introduction of Buddhism in the United States began just over one hundred years ago. There are three main branches of Buddhism: Zen, Theravadan, and Tibetan. Zen Buddhism was established first and was followed about seventy years later by Tibetan and Theravadan Buddhism. This book is primarily based on Tibetan Buddhism, the branch of Buddhism that the Dalai Lama is the icon for.

Due to the increased interest in alternatives to Judeo-Christian thought and the positive role model of the Dalai Lama, interest in Buddhism continues to expand as people examine their lives and seek to increase meaning and joy. *The Twelve Steps as a Path to Enlightenment* provides existing Buddhists and future converts a bridge between traditional Twelve Step texts, with their monotheistic world view, and the world view of Buddhism. Without the need to interpret the traditional Twelve Step texts, Buddhists will have an easier time "working the program" and gain more benefit from their efforts: freedom from compulsions, greater meaning in life, serenity and ultimate peace.

This book is not intended to be comprehensive nor provide an authoritative Buddhist way to work the steps. Indeed, although the title whimsically suggests this is "How the Buddha Works the Steps", the Buddha himself adapted his teachings to meet the needs and capacity of the people he was addressing. Likewise, this book will appeal to some, but surely not to all. Other books exist specifically for the Buddhist working a Twelve Step program and some individuals may find that another title is more informative or inspiring. Five other books that may be of interest are:

One Breath at a Time - Buddhism and the 12 Steps by Kevin Griffin, 2004

Burning Desire – Dharma, God & the Path of Recovery by K.Griffin, 2010

12 Steps on Buddha's Path - Bill, Buddha, and We by Laura S., 2006

The 12-Step Buddhist by Darren Littlejohn, 2009

The Zen of Recovery by Mel Ash, 1993

All five of these books are wonderful. What is unique about *The Twelve Steps as a Path to Enlightenment* is that it shows how the Twelve Steps can be worked from a truly Buddhist world view. This text integrates the Twelve Steps with the Buddha's path to enlightenment, resulting in a complete program.

A World View for Spiritual Seekers that Believe there is no God.

An estimated three million people worldwide practice a Twelve Step program. However, in the United States alone, over 60 million people suffer with some type of addiction or compulsive behavior they cannot control. *The Twelve Steps as a Path to Enlightenment* serves to open the door for people not in a program, since one of the main reasons that people are turned off from Twelve Step programs is the emphasis on God. Even though members are allowed to define their higher power, religious monotheism permeates most groups. Twelve Step program literature and the Twelve Steps contain many references to God and use unmistakably religious prayers of Judeo-Christian origin.

Twelve Step fellowships claim to be "spiritual and not religious". However, as soon as the word God or Higher Power is used, the program becomes a monotheistic program inadvertently excluding Buddhists and other types of spiritual people. For some of us, the attraction to other aspects of the program kept us in the rooms. For others, the subtle message that we would need to eventually believe in God left us looking for a more agreeable solution.

The Twelve Steps as a Path to Enlightenment is a guidebook that takes the teachings of the Buddha and the ancient commentaries of Indian and Tibetan Buddhist masters and translates them into the framework of the Twelve Steps, explaining how the Twelve Steps can work without belief in a God or a higher power. This book may open the doors for some people that have previously been turned off from Twelve Steps programs. It can be used as a basic text for Twelve Step focus groups that serve Buddhists.

The following features will allow more people to access the benefits of greater happiness and ease that one comes to expect from working a Twelve Step program:

- Steps are rewritten to remove references to God or Higher Power.

- How the steps work without "God" is clearly explained from the Tibetan Buddhist perspective.

- What one does to take each step using this new approach is specifically outlined.

A "Lam Rim" for Westerners

"Lam" is Tibetan for path and "rim" means steps. Together they mean the steps on the path to enlightenment. The Indian Master Atish[1]a wrote the first lam rim in the 11th century when he relocated to Tibet. In order to teach Tibetans Buddhism he needed a complete and concise summary of the entire path. Building on his work, Je Tsongkapa[2], a teacher of the first Dalai Lama, wrote a number of lam rims ranging in size from 1,000 to 2 pages.

Our problem here in the West is, while we have copies of these lam rims, they are not truly accessible. For instance, Je Tsongkapa's Lam Rim Chen Mo is 984 pages long. It has a commentary to explain it that is 1,772 pages long. Not only are many texts laboriously long, they are not modern, are written in "code", and/or they are not written for our culture.

The Twelve Steps as a Path to Enlightenment is inspired by teachings of the first westerner to complete the Geshe program of study at a Tibetan Monastery and under the guidance of Tibetan lamas. Geshe Michael Roach, after twenty-five years of study and a rigorous final public debate lasting days, graduated with the Western equivalent to a doctorate in theology. He subsequently took the lam rim teachings and translated them into language and practices that we can relate to here in the West. Based entirely upon Buddhist texts and originally taught before live audiences, these teachings are available free to the public as a series of eighteen audio courses that take roughly 700 to 1,000 hours to complete. (See Asian Classics Institute in the resource section at the end of this book.)

After studying the teachings of Geshe Michael Roach I realized that the steps on the path to enlightenment were all reflected in the spiritual principles embodied in the Twelve Steps. In other words, the Twelve Steps were a complete lam rim! This work is my attempt to provide a modern lam rim that is organized around the Twelve Step format.

---

[1] Lord Atisha(980-1054) was a great Indian Buddhist master that was brought to Tibet by the early Tibetan Buddhists to teach them.

[2] Je Tsongkapa (1357-1419) was the founder of the Ganden Monastery and the Gelug school of Tibetan Buddhism. He was a prolific writer (thousands of pages)and much of his work was inspired directly by Manjushri, the future buddha.

STEP ONE

We admitted we were powerless over what we hoped we could control – that our lives had become unmanageable.

<u>What Lies Ahead</u>

The first step on the path to enlightenment involves an honest appraisal of our way of living and goals in life. Most of us want to be happily satisfied. This can take many forms and usually involves having our basic physical needs taken care of, as well as feeling connected to others and appreciated. We want love and meaning in our lives. Freedom, autonomy and influence are other universal needs. It seems that the ability to control our world so that we can maintain our happiness is something that would be essential.

In the First Step we critically examine, with an open and curious mind, if what we are doing is really working for us. The purpose of this step is to realize that our approach to life is not completely satisfying and some, or many, of our needs go unmet. During our exploration, we may find what we are doing only works sometimes or perhaps not very frequently at all. We may also notice that something that works for others does not necessarily work for us, or vice versa. Further, some areas of our lives may seem fine, but other areas may be disappointing.

We must come to conclude, after the analysis of our life, that what we are doing does not work all the time or in all situations. If, instead, we are satisfied with our life and the future that lies ahead of us, then there is no need to do anything different. An attitude of dissatisfaction, unhappiness, or even disgust, is needed to proceed with the remaining steps. Only upon this foundation do we find we have a solid motivation for grasping a way of life that is new and novel, but ultimately effective in bringing us lasting happiness.

I want to forewarn the reader that, although the First Step can be somewhat morbid and depressing, only a complete understanding of what we will be discussing in this step can lead to the type of motivation required to complete the remaining steps. It is like the bumper sticker that states, "If you aren't angry, you're not paying attention." In this step we start to pay close attention to what is really going on in our lives. We also let go of any tendency to see good in the world and focus on the negative aspects of even a happy life as a human. Admittedly, to focus on suffering would be a miserable past-time if we did not have at our disposal a program (the Twelve Steps) that can change our future world. Here, our focus will be on taking the sugar coating off of life and looking at the cold reality of it. In Step One, we admit we cannot control anything and that our lives are unmanageable.

For people already on a spiritual path, as I suspect many of my readers will be, this step may actually be a step backward. You may have already accepted that many things about this world are negative and you cannot change them. From that place you may have already moved on to a practice that focuses on the positive in this world. This is a splendid, worthwhile world view. However, simply ignoring the negative creates a pleasant experience that is only temporary. My purpose in this writing is to show how the Twelve Steps, developed by Alcoholics Anonymous, and which have spread like wild-fire to now support people with many different types of addictions or living problems, are a complete path to end all negativity permanently.

Our Ambitious Goal

This seems like an incredible claim. Certainly, millions of people have defeated life-threatening addictions with the Twelve Steps. And many more have improved their lives dramatically with the application of the principles embodied in the steps. But to claim that one can defeat aging, sickness, depression and death with the Steps, certainly this is too much to believe! In fact, defeating death is beyond any sensible person's wildest dreams. However, that is exactly what I am saying here. The key to what the Shakyamuni Buddha taught was that all negativity can be eliminated in its entirety, never to return. With the elimination of negativity, a heavenly state arises and negative events such as aging and death cease to occur. "Heaven" is not an eternal state that can only be reached after death, but is a state that can be achieved before death – if we are to believe the Buddha. The principle steps the Buddha taught to achieve this state free from suffering mirror the spiritual principles that are inherently part of the Twelve Steps.

The elimination of negativity or mental afflictions stops the aging process and actually transforms the body. Mental afflictions are simply any thought that disturbs the mind that has that thought. These include anger, jealousy, anxiety and fear. Although science corroborates that mental afflictions, also known as stress, are a major contributor to the aging process, I think I would be hard pressed to present an argument in the limited space that would satisfy my readers that death can be stopped. The "proof" requires a thorough understanding of the law of cause and effect and many other ideas that may be foreign to my readership. It would be akin to presenting a proof for "tunneling".

Tunneling is a process by which a particle moves from one location in space to another location in space without being anywhere in between. Sounds pretty fantastic, eh? I remember exploring the proof for this in college decades ago. In order to prove such a thing I first had to learn simple arithmetic, then I learned algebra and trigonometry, and finally

> **Mental Afflictions:**
> Any thought that disturbs the mind.
> e.g. anger, jealousy, anxiety, fear, hate, sadness, yearning

calculus. With these tools and other equations of quantum physics at my hand, I was able to mathematically reason ("prove") that such a phenomenon was possible. But truth be known, all that math was not very convincing. It was the fact that people I respected told me that a particle can move from location to location without "touching" down at locations in between that allowed me to remain open to the possibility.

For people that would like to take the time to learn the "simple math, algebra and calculus" of Buddhist logic, there are courses available. I studied with the Asian Classics Institute, which offers free course materials by download at ACIdharma.org. As for whether stopping death is possible, certainly do not believe me without running it through your filters and then putting the ideas that follow into practice. Further, if that is too fantastic, (and truth be known I teeter on disbelief), then consider that the principles taught by the Buddha and embodied in the Steps might still be able to improve the quality of your life dramatically.

It is important to not accept any teaching blindly. To emphasize this point, I will repeat the words of the Buddha: "Accept my words only after you have finished a careful examination of them, testing them like gold: 1) in the fire, 2) by cutting and 3) by using the touchstone too."

The Buddha always stressed to not accept anything on blind faith. In this quote, from the Pali Canon, he uses the analogy of testing his ideas like one tests gold they want to purchase. It was standard protocol in ancient India to thoroughly test any gold before you bought it. To do this one would 1) melt a piece to see if it was pure, 2) cut some to see if there were any impurities on the inside and 3) rub another stone against it to see what mark it left as a test for purity. These tests represent, respectively, 1) checking the assertion against your own personal experience, 2) checking to see if it is sound by logical analysis ("cutting" it apart with your mind), and 3) checking if it contradicted other authorities that you trusted or believed could not lie ("rubbing" it against another source). If these tests do not provide you with conclusive evidence supporting the validity of any claim, it is still important to remain open-minded, especially to things you cannot disprove.

Who is the Buddha?

Before we proceed with one way of completing a thorough First Step, a brief description of the Buddha's background seems sensible. The Buddha was born Siddhartha Gautama about 2,500 years ago in India. When he was born it was prophesied that he would become a great leader. His leadership could take one of two forms: either he would become a great king or a great sage.

His father, the king of the Shakya clan of India, wanted his son to follow in his footsteps and so shielded him both from religious teachings and the suffering of the world. Siddhartha grew up in the lap of luxury. Surrounded only by sensual pleasures of sight, sound, taste and touch, he was completely isolated from the normal reality of the world and shielded from all signs of sickness, aging and death until he was twenty-nine.

Then, at this age, during excursions outside the palace, he encountered first a very old man, then someone overtaken with illness, then a dead body, and finally an ascetic, or spiritual renunciant. These first experiences of suffering disturbed him greatly, and eventually led him to leave his worldly life in search of a way to transcend aging, illness, and death. Six years later, through a combination of meditative practice and analysis of reality, he became enlightened.

What is Enlightenment?

Enlightenment is sometimes referred to as nirvana, "gone to bliss", or being "awakened". This term typically refers to the highest state of achievement on a spiritual path, but sometimes people use it to refer to lower states of achievement that represent milestones in the process. It is important to note that "enlightenment" in some spiritual traditions is very different from the ultimate goal of Buddhism. The technical definition of enlightenment (in Tibetan Buddhism) is: the permanent cessation of mental afflictions due to the realization of ultimate reality and the individual analysis of the Four Truths that are realized subsequent to the direct perception of ultimate reality.

Trying to give the definition in more plain language is simply impossible. Some of the characteristics of the person that is enlightened are:

- they have no more "bad" thoughts (no jealousy, anger, sadness, etc.)

- they abide in ultimate reality (We will talk about this extensively.)

- they no longer experience themselves as having a self

- their experience is extremely pleasant

The process of becoming enlightened and the description of the state of enlightenment could fill volumes of books. Further, since this state is so foreign to our normal way of existing, all the descriptions would sound more like fairy tales than possibilities. With this in mind, I will not go into the details of enlightenment more, but instead ask the reader to consider the possibility of a way of living that is completely different than what they know now. Could there be a state of living that was both blissful and lasting? Perhaps something akin to a heavenly existence? Sometimes this state is just referred to as 'peace'. In contemplating the possibility, consider all that you know, either from personal experience or from authorities you trust, about both the human mind and its potential.

> **Enlightenment** is the permanent cessation of mental afflictions.

The best modern account of the enlightenment process and description of the state of nirvana is written by Bernadette Roberts, a Christian contemplative who reached what she refers to as "no-self". In the Tibetan tradition, she would be referred to as a "self-made buddha" since her description of "no-self" matches what Tibetan's call "lower nirvana".

Tibetans recognize two "forms" of enlightenment. Lower nirvana is the state of enlightenment that occurs when a "regular" person realizes the permanent cessation of mental afflictions. Total enlightenment is the state of becoming a buddha. If a "regular" person becomes enlightened at the same time as having bodhichitta (the sincere wish to become enlightened to help all other beings) then they are transformed into a buddha in that same moment. In both cases, the nirvana that is experienced is the same. The major difference is that a buddha is also omniscient.

The Awakened State

The Buddha taught that there are two different realities going on at all times. One is a deceptive reality and the other is often referred to as ultimate reality or ultimate truth. People that are enlightened abide in ultimate reality while still having some awareness of deceptive reality. The rest of us are stuck in deceptive reality at all times.

Deceptive reality is named for the fact that the way things appear to exist and work is not the way they really are or how they really work. We are being deceived. (Hence the name deceptive reality.) The bad news is that our everyday, conventional reality is just this state. Nothing actually works the way it appears to. It is because we cannot see this that we are stuck here in this suffering realm.

Sure, occasionally we get a sense that what is happening is not getting us anywhere. We have this attitude when we refer to our working careers as being a "rat race". We might have the sense that what we invest the most energy into does not really pay off. Still, despite having this haunting awareness, we continue to run around because: 1) we do not know what else to do, 2) we want to escape from unpleasantness, and/or 3) everyone else seems to be approaching life this way. If we stand back and take an objective look, we do appear to be in a convoluted maze searching for non-existent exits.

Our First Realization Upon the Path

Before we delve into what ultimate reality is, and how knowledge of it can get us out of the maze of deceptive reality, let's take a good look at where we live. People can become enlightened as a result of perceiving ultimate reality directly during deep meditation. After their first experience of ultimate reality, they come out of their meditation and realize that everything they are seeing is deceptive.

Four Noble (Arya) Truths
(1) There is suffering
(2) Suffering has an origin
(3) Suffering has an end
(4) There is a path to end suffering

They also realize Four Truths that are the hallmark of Buddhism. These Four Truths are sometimes referred to as the Four Noble Truths or the Four Arya Truths. (The term Arya Truth is the more linguistically correct because a person that has seen ultimate reality directly is called an arya. However, due to early translations, the term Noble Truth is more commonly used.) The experience of seeing ultimate reality and realizing the Four Truths provides one with the wisdom to completely defeat all of one's mental afflictions and enter a dynamic state of everlasting bliss.

The first of the Four Truths is called the truth of suffering and it is the meat of the First Step. In his first lecture after becoming enlightened, the Buddha said the following about the First Noble Truth:

> This is the Noble Truth of suffering: birth is suffering, aging is suffering; illness is suffering; death is suffering; sorrow, lamentation, pain, grief and despair are suffering; union with what is displeasing is suffering; separation from what is pleasing is suffering; not to get what one wants is suffering; in brief, the five aggregates subject to clinging are suffering.

Let's examine this. Again our focus is not on taking a balanced view or appreciating the goodness that surrounds us. We are trying to see if we can find anything that is not spoiled by suffering:

- "Birth is suffering." True. The actual act of giving birth causes pain for both the mother and child and sometimes results in death.

- "Aging is suffering." True. No matter how healthy, the body seems to decline as one ages and gives rise to physical and mental limitations, if not to outright aches and pains.

- "Illness is suffering." True. Being sick is no fun for the person that is ill or for those around that person.

- "Death is suffering." True. Both unpleasant for the person leaving and for those that lose that person.

- "Sorrow, lamentation, pain, grief and despair" are all obvious forms of suffering.

- "Union with what is displeasing is suffering" goes hand in hand with "Separation from what is pleasing is suffering" and "not to get what one wants is suffering". If you like it cold and want it to be that temperature, and you do not like it hot, then you "suffer" when it is hot and you "suffer" when the cold (and that which you desire) ends.

- "The five aggregates subject to clinging are suffering." This is a little more obtuse. The Buddha defined a person as being made up of five aggregates. These five parts to a person are 1) physical form, 2) feelings, 3) discrimination (a.k.a. perceptions), 4) other formations, and 5) awareness (a.k.a. consciousness). Why he decided to divide a person up into these five parts is another story, but for our purposes we could view the statement as "a person subject to clinging is suffering." This is true also. This evokes the image of someone trying to hold onto something that is slipping away, like an ice cream cone on a hot, sunny day. When we cling to anything that is not everlasting, we end up suffering.

The last point above, really sums up the gist of the problem. We have the tendency to cling to the things we like. This is the essence of the Second Noble Truth – that suffering originates from our craving. This will be discussed in detail a little later in this chapter. First, let's complete the analysis of how certain aspects of the way the world works inherently cause us grief.

Is it All Really Suffering?

First let us consider the impermanent nature of our world. The obvious truth is that nothing lasts. The very basis of cyclic life (samsara in Sanskrit) is that things change. If we are born, then we surely will die. Relationships end. That person that we used to dislike, we now like. Every other year we have to get a new computer. Our record albums were replaced by 8-track tapes, which were replaced by cassettes, and then those by compact discs, and then MP3 downloads, and so on. Equipment we like we can no longer get replacement parts for. Our kids grow up and want to have nothing to do with us and then this changes and we cannot get them out of our house.

Not only is everything changing, nothing is predictable. That person we thought we would always be best friends with suddenly betrays us. We spend our life saving for retirement only to get terminal cancer at 60 years of age. A late frost kills our newly planted tomatoes. Further, even as we push to achieve something, we find that whatever we achieve is lost again. As the saying goes, "What goes up must come down". The investment strategies that worked so well, for so long, no longer give us the results we have come to count on. We get to the top of the ladder in our career only to find ourselves downsized.

What about our constant dissatisfaction? Have you ever noticed how long satisfaction lasts? When I first started working I was happy just to have a job. Years later, I was not satisfied with a huge salary, especially when I leaned that other people in the company were making more than me. This is the crux of the addiction problem: the continual search for something that will make us feel good all the time. As soon as we get the desired object we want (crave), we are off trying to achieve more or get something that is bigger and better. A careful examination of our lives will provide ample evidence of dissatisfaction even in the happiest person. The simple shifting of posture to get more comfortable is a manifestation of subtle dissatisfaction.

Many times the worst thing that can happen to someone, is that they actually get everything they have ever hoped for and what they had been working for their whole life. This is one point where we find ourselves face to face with our dissatisfied nature. I hit the wall personally just after I turned thirty years old. I had achieved a close approximation to what I wanted in life with a few remaining things close to my fingertips. I had it all! Did I reflect on it with self-satisfaction and happiness? No, it was at this point I got incredibly depressed. I had a sort of mid-life crises. At the time I was not sure why I was so down, but now I am aware that my depression was based on the realization behind the question, "This is it?" It was like I had paid all this money to see an acclaimed movie or theater show and did not even like it. What a letdown!

Thus far, we have discussed impermanence, unpredictability, and constant dissatisfaction. The worst part of all is that, according to Eastern thought, we have to do it over and over again. When we speak of cyclic life it is not just the rise and fall within one lifetime, but the fact that we are forced to be reborn again and again, and not always in the most pleasant of circumstances.

Here again, I am broaching a subject, reincarnation, that very few people have direct experience of. The Eastern belief is that the mind continues on as a stream that does not end at the physical death of the body. The mind is made of "stuff" that is invisible and aware, while the body (including the brain) is made of physical matter.

Some of you may say, "Well, I just do not believe that. Prove it!"

And to that I can only respond, "Prove to me that the mind ends when the body dies." While it does appear the mind is associated with a particular body, there is no evidence that the mind is dependent on or inseparable from the body. Indeed, the mind could very well be separate from the body and continue on after the body dies.

As we say frequently in Twelve Step programs, "Take what you like and leave the rest." This means that if some of the ideas I am presenting do not sit well with you, then only take what you think is worthwhile. Certainly consider the possibility of the ideas I am presenting, but do not get too bogged down in thinking you have to accept anything that insults your intelligence.

At this point, we are safe to conclude that everything in the realm we live in is suffering. Some things are complete misery, like pain itself. Other things are a combination of good and bad, like something we enjoy very much that we ultimately will have to part with, (either because it is lost, broken, or used up; or because we die and leave it behind). Further, we are powerless to control or avert this suffering. We are stuck.

Denial? Or Ignorance?

It is because we are stuck, along with everyone else, that we may not notice immediately that what we are doing is not working. In Twelve Step programs, the state before one admits they have a problem and takes the First Step is referred to as denial. Typically, the people around them might be thinking, "They sure have a problem with their drinking (or eating or tendency to meddle in other people's business)," while they do not see it or believe it themselves. And further, other people with the same problem will not think that the person is in denial either. An active addict may not consider the use of drugs a problem since they have a personal investment in making sure nothing threatens their own drug use.

I have never liked being told I was in denial, since to deny something is an active process. It is akin to being told the truth and then denying it. My state before finding recovery was more like just not knowing any better or thinking what I was doing was really okay or the best I could do.

In Buddhism, the state before realizing how the world works is not called denial, it is called ignorance. This does not mean that someone is stupid. It just means that someone does not know something, and in this case, something critical but also hidden. Indeed, someone can be very smart and still not really know how things work, simply because they have not examined their reality closely. Such a person has simply accepted what they were told as children or the beliefs of the people around them.

Part of our ignorance is that we do not really get that things do not last and that they change unpredictably. If we really got this on a deep level, how could we be upset when the equipment we are using breaks or our friend does not want to spend time with us today? We would expect the unexpected at all times.

What Causes Suffering?

Our problem is not the nature of our suffering world, but our reaction to it. We do not want to suffer, so we crave escape. This is the true ignorance. We believe that we can do something in the moment an unpleasantness occurs that will make it go away. For instance, the moment our back goes out we "know" that if we just would have stretched that morning it would not have happened. We think that focusing on that idea (or a similar "solution") that we would be pain free. Instead, because of this craving for a different result, we create more suffering. In our example of back pain, we have added mental anguish on top of the physical pain we are already dealing with.

In an extreme example of how our craving escape causes more suffering, the addict that wishes to have more of their drug of choice may kill, steal and lie to get more. In a milder example, it is the energy and time (in the form of arguments) that is wasted on getting the office building a "perfect" temperature when no two people can agree what that "perfect" temperature would be.

The Buddha recognized the suffering inherent in life and speculated that there must be a way to end it, permanently. Making sure everyone is fed, child abuse is stopped, or the world climate is controlled, will not end all suffering. In order to end all suffering, which he believed was indeed possible, he needed to find its cause. His investigation involved tracing suffering back moment by moment to see what caused it.

When we start this process ourselves, we first find that things and conditions are not necessarily suffering all by themselves. The earthquake that destroys one person's home creates prosperity in another person's home, since they sell something in high demand in the earthquake's aftermath. The doctor who kills someone accidentally, also saves someone else's life. The color I like, you hate. The statement I take offense at, does not bother you in the least.

The first thing we can conclude is that suffering does not come from some inherently "suffering" external thing, but seems to be dependent on our internal view. Suffering is not "out there". It is a personal thing.

In order to investigate the internal mind space, training in meditation is required. One must be able to fix the mind on the object of its investigation and stay focused without drifting. When the Buddha left his palace, he first sought out instruction in meditation in order to train his mind to the level that would be needed to investigate the nature of suffering. Once he was able to reach this level of concentration, he proceeded to try to destroy the propensity to suffer by exposing himself to harsh practices, including starvation. The plan was to learn to transcend suffering by exposing oneself to pain and learning how not to feel it.

That path did not work and he eventually discarded it. He opted at that point to sit down and take a good long look at what was going on. With a level of concentration that requires extensive training and is quite rare today, he turned his mind on suffering. What he learned is expressed as the Second Noble Truth:

> This is the Noble Truth of the origin of suffering: It is craving which produces rebirth, bound up with pleasure and greed. It finds delight in this and that; in other words, craving for sense pleasures, craving for existence or becoming and craving for nonexistence or self-annihilation.

Is Our Problem Craving?

Is craving at the root of all our problems? Let's take a look. When our car breaks down, why do we get upset? Are we upset because we want something? It appears so. At a basic level, we want our life to go smoothly. We think we have to have the car running well, right now! If we are on our way someplace important, perhaps we do not want to disappoint someone or lose our job. We are craving that the unpleasantness ends. Attachments that get us in trouble are often expressed in the form of "I have to..." or "I should...". A good question to ask yourself is what would happen if you did not do that thing you think you have to?

This is the opportunity for personal investigation. Whenever you are uncomfortable, upset or suffering, look for the cause underneath. Are you wishing something would be different? Can you find even one instance when this is not the case? It is a very simple truth that craving and attachment cause suffering, and it may seem quite obvious, but we slip into the trap over and over. Knowing the immediate cause of unhappiness can provide a way to experience less of it in the short run.

It is the fact that we struggle against things we cannot change, at the moment they happen, that makes our life unmanageable. Once the car accident occurs, we cannot "undo" it. Getting angry at the other driver only spoils our own peace of mind further. The great Indian Buddhist Master, Shantideva, gives the following advice:

> If there is something you can do about it, why get upset?
>
> If there is nothing you can do about it, what is the use in getting upset?

While it seems perfectly natural to become unhappy when something undesirable happens (like grieving the loss of a loved one), we can also see our unhappiness is proportionate to our attachment. When a beloved relative dies, we are very sad and remain so for a long time. When a relative we do not care about dies, we enjoy the snacks at the wake and go home happy to have spent time with people we care about.

I am not suggesting we repress our natural feelings of loss. That would be akin to the Buddha's attempt to transcend suffering by starving and then ignoring the pain and discomfort. My intention here, in Step One, is to point out first that greater attachment does lead to greater suffering. When the beloved is lost, be it a person, animal, dream, or object, we will naturally grieve. My second point is that we also tend to create suffering over our suffering by not accepting the loss. This lack of acceptance can take the form of blaming ourselves for not being more careful or considerate, or blaming others for being negligent or inconsiderate.

Completing Step One

Acceptance is a key spiritual principle embodied in the First Step. The greater our ability to accept things as they are and accept that we have very little power over things, the quicker our ability to realize true peace. In Step One, we admit we cannot really control our lives, at least not how we thought we should be able to. We realize our future prospects are not so great unless we can find another way of doing things that really works.

This admission of "defeat" is not a place we then spend the rest of our lives in. The qualifier is that we cannot control things the way we thought we could up to now. We learn that what we were told by society, e.g. work hard and succeed, does not necessarily lead to happiness or even success.

In the First Step, we affirm the truth that things are not going as well as we want and turn our backs on our old ways. We are only powerless until we learn a new way of being in the world and relating to the world. We are now ready to move to the Second Step where our work is to envision the possibility of our lives filled with more meaning, joy, and, perhaps even, eternal bliss.

STEP TWO
Came to believe that we could know peace.

The next step, after admitting that things are not working, is imagining the possibility of a way that things could work that is not based on the methods we have used in the past. This reasoning is really quite simple and follows naturally after the First Step. Once we determine that our current prospects are less than satisfying, we either come to believe that there is another way, or we surrender to acceptance that we cannot expect anything better and remain in despair.

The traditional wording of this step is "came to believe that a Power greater than ourselves could restore us to sanity." Although the Twelve Step literature suggests that the power can be anything outside of oneself, including the fellowship of the group or an inanimate object, the use of a capital "P" in the word Power hints to an identifiable, self-existent God. This is one of the major stumbling blocks for many people in being able to use and embrace the Twelve Steps as a way of living.

I prefer dropping the reference to a higher power because it allows me more freedom to see the divine (meaning spiritual or anything that uplifts my spirit) in mundane objects outside myself as well as in thoughts and feelings that appear to arise from within me. It also removes the subtle reference to the religious concept of a monotheistic god, which detracts from the Twelve Steps as a spiritual program. The use of the word God and monotheistic concepts immediately shifts the Twelve Steps into a religious framework, and out of a spiritual framework since these ideas are not unique to all spiritual paths or religions.

Our Goals for Step Two

There are two things we must accomplish with Step Two. First we need to have a belief that our life could be better and second we need to believe that there is a way to make that happen. (That "way" to improve our life would be the "higher power".) At this point, we do not have to believe that our life will improve, only that there is a plausible way for our life to improve.

What are Beliefs Anyway?

Before we get into the tasks of cultivating new beliefs, let's first consider what a belief is and where our beliefs come from. A belief is something we accept as true or real without absolute proof. We tend to have a variety of beliefs that we hold with varying levels of certainty. For instance, someone may believe that when they let the cat outside to play it will not wander off. Or if it does, that it will eventually come back. This belief guides their actions: they willingly let the cat they value outside to play. Or someone may believe that saturated fats are bad for them. Again this belief either motivates them to avoid saturated fats or to think they are doing something bad each time they eat them. One last example would be the belief that jumping off the top of a ten-story building will lead to death. This belief is held so strongly by many of us that very few test it unless we are counting on just that result.

> A **belief** is something we accept as true or real without absolute proof.

Frequently, beliefs are tied to judgments. That fats are bad is one such example. We may also believe that good people do not tell lies or that lying sometimes, such as a 'white lie', is okay.

Some of our beliefs were given to us by our parents. For instance, I was taught that people of certain nationalities had characteristics of being dumb or lazy, that if a man cheated on his wife it was her fault, and it was not okay to harass animals. More subtle beliefs that can be handed down would be what makes a person worthy, like "my worth is dependent on how well I serve my parents (or partner or kids)".

Many of my personal beliefs reflect my personal values. Recycling plastic is good. Throwing away leftover food is bad. Being on time for appointments is good. I could go on and on.

Once a belief is created, it is often held like a fixed and solid thing. We easily forget how arbitrary beliefs are and what goes into their creation, especially beliefs about how the world works from a spiritual perspective. Many of us simply do not think to actively examine the beliefs that came to us during our childhood until we bump into some that are limiting us or causing us problems. Then, once we examine them and find that they do not really hold up to logical reasoning, we can become more open to exploring our other ideas that might be mistaken. I mean, why is it a woman's fault when a man cheats on her?

My first sponsor in program was a fundamentalist Christian. She believed there was a true and absolute God. Her perspective was that this God was too large and complex to be known by us. She would use the parable of the blind men and the elephant to illustrate how the many religions and spiritual beliefs could all be 100% right.

In the parable, a group of blind men examine an elephant to learn what it is like. One decides it is like a wall. Another claims it is like a pillar. The others say "No, it is a spear... a fan... or a rope", each depending upon where they touched. In the story, the group goes on to argue amongst themselves about who is right. This is much like those of us that would try to describe God or an ultimate reality that defies conception. Perhaps we are all correct and yet incomplete?

The story reminds me not to hold to any of my beliefs too rigidly, since I might not have the full picture. Given there are so many things that are beyond my personal experience (remember the definition of a belief is something I cannot know for sure), I test the beliefs that are important to me. The acid test for the usefulness of a belief is how it affects my life when I act as if it is true. In short, does it make my life better? With this said, I am not going to invest a lot of energy deciding whether fairies exist or not because, at least for today, the existence of fairies will not affect my actions and therefore will not impact my life significantly.

In my investigation of useful beliefs, I like to follow the same method that science uses for validating beliefs. In science, the process starts with someone getting an idea that something is true. This idea is called a hypothesis. It could also be referred to as something they believe. They test their idea and either disprove it or find that it holds true. They may then tell other people (publish in a scientific journal) and others may go on to test it themselves. At a certain point the original idea or a refined variation of that idea may become accepted by many and reach the rank of a theory. A theory in this situation is an idea that has been tested and scrutinized. If the theory holds the test of time and seems to be consistently valid, it may reach the level of a law.

When a belief reaches the level of a law is it proven true? No, this is one of the misunderstandings people have about scientific laws and scientific truths. The scientific method can never prove anything absolutely. It is really good at disproving things, but universal proof simply is not possible. We can only say that the evidence supports a specific law or belief. It is always possible that Newton's apple will not fall on the third Thursday of April in the year 3035, thereby showing that the law of gravity is not a law, but only a condition of our times.

Beliefs are Different from Truth

My point with this discussion is to illustrate that a belief is not the same as a truth. I find it most useful to hold my beliefs loosely and consider them models that I live by. I act as if my model works and then examine my life for results. Not exactly a scientific experiment, but I am not concerned about discovering what will work for everyone, just what will work for me at this time in my life.

For instance, taking arnica will always reduce muscle soreness after hard exercise and bruising after I have suffered a blow. I think it is amazing. Does it work for everyone? Apparently not. I have offered it to some people and they have not gotten the same results. The literature on homeopathic medicine suggests that homeopathic arnica would be counteracted by mint and coffee. Perhaps this is the reason it does not work for my friends. Do I stop using it just because it does not work for everyone? No! It still works for me.

I have one criteria for a belief being useful: [does it bring me more peace?] Peace is my personal ultimate goal. Your goal may be different. When I adopt a belief, I am not as concerned about whether it reflects "ultimate truth" as much as I am about the results it produces in my life.

For example, when I read the research that "proved" feverfew does not work as an alcohol extract I believed it. This belief led me to stop taking the feverfew extract I had been using to reduce my migraine headaches. When my headaches came back and subsequently went away when I started using feverfew again, I changed my belief about the validity of that study. I also changed my belief in the value of scientific research for determining personal truth.

It is truly wonderful how malleable beliefs can be. It really helps me to simplify things by having the "belief filter" that asks, "Will acting on this belief bring me more peace or not?" as opposed to having a belief filter that asks, "What is right or true?" Ultimately, it makes sense that what is right and true will bring me more peace, but it is easier to determine if I am peaceful than if I am "right". And I daresay that going after peace and being loving and gentle with myself, even if my actions may be "morally" wrong, will naturally lead me to greater wholeness, and with that an ability to live ethically without effort or strain.

One last thought on beliefs. Even though one of my intentions for writing this book is to give an alternate view on the Twelve Steps that is not based on a Higher Power that can be called God, I admit that I have used what I call the "God model" for many years in specific circumstances since it seems to give me good results. I do not believe that there is a self-existent god that is omnipotent, but I find that when I ask for help I often get guidance. Where this 'help' comes from does not matter to me, although I do have my own beliefs about the matter. What is important to me is that the method works for me. It brings me more peace. I am interested in results, not philosophy.

Can You Imagine a Better Life?

Now back to the work of the Second Step. As mentioned earlier, we need to create a belief that our life could be better and also a belief that there is a way for that to happen.

The first task is fairly straightforward. Do you believe that your life could be better? In Step One, we considered all the ways our life was not working for us. It is a natural progression to imagine that the trouble areas of our lives could be improved.

Perhaps you believe that your life could get better, but just not that one problem area. Your belief is good enough for Step Two, but you may want to do further investigation around why you believe your problem area can not improve. Is it true that no one with your problem has overcome it? I look around me for people that appear to not have the troubles I have. These people prove to me that it is possible to live without the problems I am experiencing. To fortify my belief that I can be free of my afflictions, like addiction for example, I am *not* inspired by people that have never had an addiction. My inspiration comes from those that have beaten their addiction.

We can find examples of people who have overcome many things such as addiction, childhood abuse, poverty, depression, grief associated with lost loves, as well as stress associated with hardship, both inside and outside of Twelve Step rooms. Within the rooms, as we listen to people share their stories, we hear amazing histories. One woman in a Twelve Step fellowship that used to have bill collectors calling daily is married now and about to purchase her first home – based on her good credit. Another woman in a business suit at a Twelve Step meeting used to be homeless, but now has just finished her degree in alcoholism counseling.

Likewise, in the popular literature we can find examples of the possibility of an improved life. If for some reason you cannot believe that your trouble could be less, just start looking for someone that was in a similar situation and has overcome their troubles. Once again, I need to reiterate that you do not need to believe that your life *will* get better - only that it **_could_** get better. Can you find logical proof that your life, even your trouble areas, could get better?

A Way to a Better Life

Now let us consider the second task. That is, cultivating a belief that there is a way to make our life better. In the original wording of Step Two, we are asked to believe that there is a higher power that can restore us to sanity. For our purposes it is better to phrase it as I just did. We need to believe that there is a way, method, or a series of steps that can improve our life.

If you believe there is a way (and why else would you be going to a Twelve Step meeting or reading this book?), you have completed the Second Step. However, this is a good point to spend a little more time examining the method we hope will bring us to sanity. In program literature we might find a lengthy discussion regarding what God is at this point.

In the traditional Twelve Step literature, a higher power is given as the solution to our troubles. If God is the answer, then the "cause" of our crazy life is drifting away from this higher power. This is alluded to by common program phrases such as "spiritual disease" and "disease of self-will run riot". Each specific program in its literature (usually Step One) goes into the mystery of the cause of each specific disease. Why one chooses alcohol, or drugs, or food, or sex, or love, or gambling over some other possible addictive behavior may be a mystery, but the cure is the same. This suggests that disconnection from a higher power is the underlying cause of each addiction.

For those of us that do not adhere to a belief in a higher power that can save us, we are left with the short stick at this point. We are told to act as if, which does work, but left me feeling somewhat out of place in the fellowship rooms. Our task is to determine, by a new, spiritual line of reasoning, what method will restore us to sanity and allow us to have lasting inner peace.

In Step One we discovered that our life was out of balance, insane, a mess, or simply dissatisfactory. We learned that life is suffering (First Noble Truth) and the craving is the cause of suffering (Second Noble Truth). At the beginning of Step Two we came to believe that our life could be restored to balance. Which is, in a sense, the embodiment of the Third Noble Truth. As the Buddha stated:

> This is the Noble Truth of the cessation of suffering. It is the complete cessation of suffering, the giving up, renouncing, relinquishing, detaching from craving.

Great, so all we have to do is give up craving and life will be fine. I throw my hands up in disbelief.

If we could give up craving, none of us would be in this predicament! Luckily, the Buddha taught how to accomplish this "renouncing of craving". That is the Fourth Noble Truth about the path leading to the cessation of suffering, which will be discussed in Step Three. Our job in Step Two is to believe that the end of suffering is possible.

What the Still Suffering Human Needs to Know

Now, in order to have faith in a method to improve our life, we must first identify the cause of our situation. When a possible cause is identified, the method for correcting things becomes obvious and our efforts more effective. Without identifying the proper cause, our work could be futile. It would be like trying to keep a boat afloat on a rainy day by hanging a tarp up to block the rain, while it filled with water due to a good-sized hole in the bottom. The tarp keeps the rain from filling the boat with water, but water will come in regardless. This solution might delay the end, but unless we address the hole we are doomed to sink.

Luckily, those that have gone before us have found that the spiritual principles embodied in the Steps are quite effective with saving and improving the lives of alcoholics and those with other addictive behaviors. Given our basic belief structure, we need to strip the "God" part away and focus on the spiritual principles. Once we have identified what causes our life to be good or bad, or at least have accepted what is not producing good results (Step One), and are willing to try a different approach, we can then make a decision (Step Three) to adopt a manner of living that *does* work and then proceed to begin following this manner of living (steps Four through Twelve).

Our first task in discovering what will give us the results we want, is to consider what is causing our life to unfold as it does. Here, we once again need to look a little deeper than we may be accustomed to. It is not enough to think, "I lost my job because I was absent from work a lot due to illness last year." We need to dig down layer after layer, "Why was I getting sick so much?" If the answer was I could not get the medicine that prevents the flu, whether that is the flu shot or echinacea for you, then the next question would be, "Why couldn't I get the medicine when I needed it?" and so forth.

This type of examination of the events on my life always deepens my awareness of how powerless I am over my life. It gives me a great appreciation of the complexity of life. Even something as simple as what I am having for breakfast can be seen to relate to a myriad of other things including availability of food, availability of time, exposure to breakfast food choices, childhood experiences, culture, etc. Just analyzing a breakfast choice could take all day. It certainly appears that the workings of life are a mystery and quite complex.

Who is in Charge?

Surprisingly, when we consider an overall causal agent for our life, there are only three general prospects that might be responsible for the situation we find ourselves in:

- It is all random.

- A controller being (God) is in charge.

 We control the way our life unfolds.

Let's consider each in turn.

First, perhaps the happenings of our life are just random. This is certainly a possibility. However, it is a complete dead end spiritually. If the things that happen in life are completely random, then our only hope to achieve real peace and happiness is that we get lucky. This is a pretty poor prospect.

The second possibility is that there is some controller being running our life. For me, this would be a bleak prospect also. Only a sadist controller being could have orchestrated the severe abuse I experienced as a small child. Many of us have had personal experiences that suggest there is not a compassionate being in charge that is all-powerful. One may be able to reframe events and realize the positive growth opportunities in tragic situations, but can you imagine yourself, if you were in charge, allowing cruelty so people you love and care deeply about can learn a lesson? A kind controller being running this world would certainly be the "great mystery".

Disproving a compassionate controller being overseeing the world does not eliminate the possibility of other seen or unseen 'helper' beings. Many spiritual traditions acknowledge the existence of angels, enlightened beings, and/or deities that can have some influence on our state of affairs. It is not my intention to affirm or disprove the existence of such beings. For me, they fall into the same category as a kind friend or helpful relative. They can help me and often make things better, but ultimately they are not all-powerful.

That leaves only one alternative. We have control over our destiny. I think this is a comfortable idea for many of us. It is the very simple scientific proposition that all things are a result of what caused them. The cause and effect model is the cornerstone of Western scientific thought. We test things out because we believe that the world is constructed in an organized manner that includes a certain level of predictability. Further, it is believed that if we can discover the cause(s) of something, we can affect the result.

It is the causes that have us baffled, as we saw in our analysis in Step One. For instance, I was taught one needs to work to make money. Yet further examination reveals that some people make money without working. And other people do not make money even though they worked to earn money. (Like when the company my friend worked for went into default and never paid him.) We can think of many situations when we did something expecting one result and yet another result occurred. Indeed, in Twelve Step programs, insanity is fondly referred to as *doing the same thing over and over and expecting different results.*

So if things do not work as they appear, how do they work?

Karma - The Law of Cause and Effect

The Eastern answer is that the world operates under the law of cause and effect. This law can be referred to in Sanskrit as karma. The word karma literally means "action" and, in its simplest interpretation, it means that any action or deed you do plants a mental potential (karmic seed) in your mind that later will ripen into a similar action or deed.

Karma follows four basic principles:

1 All actions lead to a result of similar type.

2 The consequences are greater than the original action.

3 If you experience something you must have done the causal action in the past.

4 Once you do the action the result cannot be lost. (But you can take action to remove it.)

For example, if you get mad at someone and shout at them, you plant the seed of anger and yelling in your mindstream. Later, you may find yourself in a situation where someone constantly is getting angry at you and shouting at you. (Or you may find yourself repeating the angry behavior again and again, even when you do not want to.) The law of karma suggests that one's previous anger and shouting plants a karmic seed or mental potential to experience angry people shouting in the future. The principles of karma further purport that if someone gets angry at you and shouts then you *must* have done something similar in the past.

Karma works as a method for creating our world in partnership with the concept of emptiness. Emptiness is the potential held in each thing that allows it to be viewed based on our karma. We will explain emptiness in greater detail during our discussion of Step Six, but we already touched on this concept during our Step One discussion when we discovered that there was no such thing as a self-existent unpleasant object. Based on that discussion, we learned that things seem bad or good only from the point of view of the viewer and do not inherently have the quality of goodness or badness. We refer to this as objects (people, places or things) being "empty" of the quality of bad or good.

For instance, one of my family members has the tendency to tell me things about the rest of the family, such as who is sick or out of work. This person thinks he is doing everyone a great service by keeping us connected. I experience this behavior as interfering with my relationships with the other family members.

The actual behavior is empty. It is simply this person talking. My karma causes me to experience it as unpleasant and that creates a desire in me to avoid talking to him. On the other hand, other family members like that he does this and actually seek him out to relay information that they do not want to convey directly to other family members.

What do I do if I want to stop hearing this person's gossip? I can tell you right off that asking him to not to talk about other family members does not work. I have repeated myself a dozen times and still he slips into his reporting behavior time and time again. If we consider my experience from a karmic perspective, then we see that the cause for hearing gossip is to have participated in gossiping in the past. For me, this is true. Twenty years ago I did tend to talk about co-workers with other co-workers.

However, it is not always possible to identify a connection to past behavior. I do not worry about that problem, since the key thing is that once I know how things arise, I can consciously manipulate my future. If I want to not hear gossiping I do not keep asking the person gossiping to stop. What I do is actively avoid anything remotely gossipy – with either positive or negative content – and I consciously say only positive comments to others. This sets up the karma to both not hear gossip and only hear pleasant things. Further, undertaking my changed behavior *purposely* potentiates the results so that they are experienced sooner.

We will explore the principles of karma further as we continue through the Steps. Although it is a keystone in Buddhism, right off you can find examples of its failure. For instance, I never molested anyone and yet was molested as a child. Indeed, to many people this idea of karma is as credible as a creator being.

The first obstacle to accepting the law of karma is that it only works well in a model that includes multiple lifetimes. Meaning, that even though I have not molested anyone in this lifetime, my molestation as a child was the result of something I did in a past life. Our inability to see past lives makes the full implications of this law hard to accept.

Indeed, some people are outright offended by the ideas of karma since it seems this means that they "deserve" the mistreatment they receive. Others point out that it pardons perpetrators, by saying, in effect, "It is the victim's karma to be mistreated, making the perpetrator innocent of offense."

Personally, if my choices for the cause of things that happen in my life are: random, God, or karma, I choose the karmic explanation simply because it implies I can affect my future.

That is the key to the cause and effect model. I have power over my future. Whatever is happening in the moment is a fruition of past karma that we are completely powerless over. It might as well be random. In fact, if the model is correct, and the karma we experience can come from countless lifetimes, then from our limited perspective it does appear random. I can imagine that I have killed and been killed countless times. I have loved and given and helped countless times too. There is an infinite pool of karma to draw upon in creating the events of my life.

An Easier Softer Explanation for Cause and Effect

What about the sun coming up in the morning? Is that a result of my personal karma? To the Mahayana school of Buddhist thought the answer is yes. However, there is another alternative view in Buddhism of the law of cause and effect. To avoid getting caught up in arguments requiring a proof of past lives and other unseen things, the law of cause and effect can actually be broken down into five different categories which may ease the mind not accepting of past lives. These are:

- Cause and effect of heredity and seeds (Bija)

- Cause and effect of seasonal changes, climate and physical inorganic order (Utu)

- Cause and effect related to electrical and magnetic forces (movement of tides, etc.) (Dharma)

- Cause and effect which governs the consciousness and will of mind (Citta)

- Cause and effect of one's actions and thoughts (Karma)

This presentation of the law of cause and effect allows for alternative causal agents besides one's past deeds. So many things that happen in your life, including your predisposition to illness, could be "caused" by heredity. Your life may be influenced by things like the external environment and your personality, both of which would be "caused" by things other than karma as presented above. In this model of the law of cause and effect, your past deeds do not "cause" you to get mugged. Karma only influences your experience of that event.

At this point you might exclaim, "Wait a minute! Slow down here! I can believe that everything in my life is directly from my own karma? Or I can think that the sun coming up is a different form of cause and effect and my karma only influences my experience of it as pleasant or unpleasant? Well, which one is true?"

This brings us back to the elephant and the blind men. Let's not be too concerned about ultimate truth, but instead focus on adopting useful beliefs that will move us toward our goals and a deeper understanding about how things work. Keep it simple and start where you are, whether that be the head of the elephant or the rear. Eventually, as we progress, we will realize the "whole elephant" or ultimate truth.

Perhaps you are thinking now, "If it does not matter if one's beliefs are an exact representation of "truth" then I could just as well believe in God."

Yes, God will work. You can take a door knob to be your higher power and still find that by working the remainder of the Twelve Steps your life will be transformed. In Step Two, our task is to believe our life can be improved and to believe there is a way for that to happen. As we proceed to live a spiritual life, our understanding of what works (our "higher power") will develop and change. And, despite my winded discussion, we are not commissioned in Step Two to define how we will be restored to sanity or come to have inner peace. We just need to come to believe there is a possibility.

Further, while this step is not about describing the method for reaching a sane and balanced life, most people need to develop a rational picture of how their lives could improve before they can "believe" they can have a better life. Indeed, once you find a model that resonates for you, then the remaining work becomes easier. If you have doubts or reservations regarding the path, these will hold you back.

The good news is that while the absence of doubt will make your work easier, having doubt is not a deal killer. Think of it as walking across a frozen lake. If you know the lake is frozen solid (since you walked on it yesterday and the temperature has remained below zero), you will move swiftly. If, however, you are not sure if it is frozen solid, you will proceed slower and more carefully, looking ahead and contemplating each step. In either case, you will reach the other side and be successful in doing so.

Why use a Karma Model?

The karmic model provides us with one possible method for developing a life that will be more satisfying, fulfilling and joyful. At a basic form it can be stated as, "as you sow, so shall you reap". This can mean that planting a kindness seed by doing some small kindness will ultimately come back to you as a lot of kindness when that seed ripens into its full form. The karmic model also provides a conceptual framework for explaining how enlightenment is possible.

Veterans in program often work through the steps periodically in order to deepen their growth. As we work the program, our capacity to grow increases along with the beneficial results our efforts have given us. When many of us first started program, Step Two was the point where we kindled some hope that the day to day insanity of our life would end. "If we could just stay away from our drug of choice or that maladaptive behavior," we thought, "we would be happy".

As we cycle through the Steps again and again, the insanity spoken of in Step Two becomes more and more subtle. To the outsider or newcomer, we may look like we have it completely together. We know, however, the subtle insanity that goes on inside. Perhaps there is a person at work or a relative at home that totally drives us batty. When faced with Step Two we may ponder "Is it possible for our method (higher power) to bring us peace in this area as well?"

Yes, according to the spiritual principles of Buddhism, it is possible to become free of even minor sufferings and discomfort. Indeed, it is possible to completely change our world into one of pure bliss. This is the promise of enlightenment. It was what the Buddha taught.

I have yet to hear enlightenment (or the end to suffering) as a goal of the Twelve Step program, even though all the steps necessary are inherently part of the Twelve Step program. The party line in fellowship is "accept life on life's terms." On a personal level, being able to accept what life gives me was a valuable step in maturing as an individual. I learned how to see the good in everything and make lemonade when presented with lemons. This is a process called reframing, and we will go into it in detail when we reach Step Six and Step Seven.

> **Reframing** is an intellectual process by which a negative situation is viewed in such a way to give it a positive meaning.

Reframing is nice, but face it, I have enough lemonade and would like to stop getting lemons. After seventeen years in program, I heard a Buddhist teacher (Geshe Michael Roach) speak about the possibility of creating a world where I could stop experiencing shit instead of just having equanimity or serenity when it happens. I was immediately interested.

As your typical human being, I want to be happy all the time. I came to Twelve Step programs thinking that if I practiced these principles in my life I could obtain this state of stable joy. Then I was taught that being happy all the time was not possible. Fortunately, I learned that the Buddha taught how to stop the lemons from coming and create happiness that does not end.

The steps to enlightenment, as taught by the Buddha, are embodied in the Twelve Steps. Our Twelve Steps are what is referred to in Tibetan Buddhism as a complete Lam Rim. (Rim = steps and Lam = Path. Together: Steps on the Path to Enlightenment)

A primary goal of mine in writing this book is to turn the world on to the fact that the Twelve Steps can not only be used without the concept of a higher power, but also can be used to create personal happiness and peace that does not end. It may seem a little far out there for most, but I would feel amiss if I did not include in Step Two a mention of being restored to what I consider true sanity. True sanity is not having any mental afflictions like anger, jealously, fear, etc. True sanity is abiding in a place of peace and happiness.

Completing Step Two

You have completed Step Two if you simply believe that there is a possibility that your life could improve dramatically for the better. You do not need to believe that it will happen, only that is possible. Once you have that belief, you are ready to move on to Step Three, where you make a decision to take on a new way of living that will lead to the life you want.

STEP THREE
Made a decision to turn our will and our lives over.

Once we have a path or method that we believe may work for us, the decision to pursue it (Step Three) follows naturally. We simply decide to give the path a try. In fact, we may find that we had already made the decision to give this new approach a try as soon as we walked into a Twelve Step fellowship room or picked up this book. Sure, we may find that as we learn more, the program is not the right thing for us and then decide to stop. Just because we make a decision to give it a try, does not mean that we cannot subsequently decide to try something else.

The traditional wording of Step Three is "Made a decision to turn our will and our lives over to the care of God as we understand him". The simple modification we make, in our non-theistic approach, is to eliminate the reference to God. Although a substitution for "God" is possible, as we shall explore later in this discussion, the emphasis in this step is surrender. We get the results we want by surrendering our old ways and adopting new, spiritual ways. Certainly we would not do this unless we were dissatisfied with our lives (Step One) and convinced that we could have a better life (Step Two).

Where Do We Turn For Refuge?
Step Three is about taking refuge. Refuge is a state of mind where one naturally turns to some outside object or person with the hope that they can offer some help. For instance, when a child is being harassed by another child they automatically will look for a teacher, parent or other ally to end their suffering. They are taking refuge in this other person to offer them some assistance. In the traditional presentation of this step, one takes refuge in God or a higher power. In our disease state we took refuge in our addiction or drug of choice.

29

In Buddhism, one takes refuge in the Three Jewels: The Buddha, the Dharma, and the Sangha. In fact, it is this act of refuge that defines a Buddhist. A Buddhist twelve-stepper believes specifically that any one or all of the three jewels may offer protection from their addiction. A Buddhist, in general, turns to the Buddha, Dharma or Sangha for assistance in ending all of their own and others' suffering.

The Three Jewels can be conceptualized in an apparent or symbolic form and in an ultimate form. The apparent form of each of the Jewels is its physical manifestation or representation. This would be the Buddha and images of the Buddha, the Dharma (the teachings of enlightened beings) in the form of books and oral transmissions, and the Sangha in the form of the monks, nuns and ordained lay people that form a Buddhist community. The ultimate form refers to how a Jewel is related to emptiness.

The Buddha Jewel

The Buddha Jewel refers to fully enlightened beings. They have followed the path that we are describing and reached its ultimate end. I say ultimate end because it is possible to become enlightened, meaning realize a permanent cessation of mental afflictions, without becoming a buddha. Being enlightened means abiding in a state of bliss free from mental afflictions. This state is sometimes referred to as nirvana. People that have reached this state are referred to as arhats or enemy-destroyers. (The enemy that is destroyed is our useless thoughts and compulsions.) While all buddhas are arhats not all arhats are buddhas.

Buddhas are referred to as fully enlightened beings because they have reached nirvana under the influence of bodhichitta. Bodhichitta is, in brief, the wish to reach total enlightenment for the benefit of all living beings. Bodhichitta springs from a sincere wish to end the suffering of all others and the realization that the best way to do this would be to reach total enlightenment or buddhahood. It is the intent of the aspiring bodhisattva (a person that has this wish) that creates the causes for buddhahood.

Buddhas, in addition to having a permanent cessation of mental afflictions, have omniscience (the ability to see the past, present, and future times simultaneously with all places) and the ability to emanate bodies spontaneously to help people in need anywhere. Our ability to receive the help of enlightened beings is only limited by our karma. Our belief in enlightened beings (specifically, a belief in their ability to help), improves our chances of being helped.

Buddhas realize these extra powers of buddhahood based on the same cause and effect model that explains how enlightened beings can help us. Bodhisattvas working towards the goal of helping all living sentient beings accumulate incredible merit (good karma) that then ripens into attributes that allow them to help all other living beings when they reach nirvana. It is the intention along with the actions that potentiate the results of the actions.

Since buddhas exist because of their commitment to help us, taking refuge in them makes sense. The extent they are able to help us is only limited by our own karma. However, the act of going to them for protection and/or assistance increases their ability to help. Sort of like, "Ask and you shall receive."

Are buddhas omnipotent?

No. For example, when the members of the Shakya clan were under attack by the ruler of Kosala, they ran to Buddha for protection. They were slaughtered even though they were in his presence. While the Buddha was not harmed, he had no power to save his people from a fate that was determined by their karma.

In addition, the buddhas, as beings that have ended their own suffering, become perfect mentors for the person aspiring to do the same. Going to the Buddha for refuge is much like a newcomer taking refuge by asking an old-timer to sponsor them. In program, our sponsors and recovery partners are an important form of refuge. In times when they are not available, we can ask for assistance from a buddha. Guidance can come from many different sources.

The Sangha Jewel

The Sangha Jewel refers to anyone that has perceived emptiness (ultimate reality) directly. A person that has perceived ultimate reality is called an arya or stream-enterer. They are referred to as stream-enterers because once you have the direct perception of emptiness it is like you are on a conveyer belt or in a stream that ends in nirvana. Taking refuge in someone that has already realized an important part of the path to enlightenment makes sense. Again, this is like taking refuge in someone that has what we want by asking them to sponsor us in learning how to obtain it for ourselves.

The Dharma Jewel

The Dharma Jewel refers to the teaching of enlightened beings. Specifically, it would be anything that provides instruction in how to progress towards enlightenment. The literature of Twelve Step programs would be included in this. I guess that makes Bob, Bill, Lois, and Anne (founding members of Alcoholics Anonymous and Al-Anon) buddhas. This is highly likely. Since buddhas have the power to emanate bodies everywhere and anytime without us knowing, anyone could be a buddha. Think about it. How could you prove otherwise?

The Dharma Jewel can be divided into two aspects. One is taking refuge in the realizations or cessations one gains from practice and the other is taking refuge in the path itself. Let's consider examples of each in detail.

About ten years into program I went through my "angry" period. Anger is the antithesis of peace. And, as I have mentioned before, peace is what I am really after. Anger is certainly not something I want to experience on a regular basis. Further, as we know from the big book of Alcoholics Anonymous, "... If we were to live, we had to be free of anger. The grouch and the brainstorm were not for us. They may be the dubious luxury of normal men, but for alcoholics these things are poison." (*Alcoholics Anonymous Big Book* Fourth Edition, page 66.)

This is how it used to be for me: I would leave my daughter in line at the sandwich counter while I did some other shopping. When I returned, it was obvious they had been skipping over her because she was just a kid. The flash of anger would be immediate and overwhelming. I would see red and make a scene. In addition, I would keep the anger going long after leaving the store by replaying the incident over and over again in my mind and by adding judgments like "they are inconsiderate or stupid". Subliminal ideas about how they ruined my plan to get out of the store quicker also fueled my fury. If I said something rude or was unpleasant during the event, I had to keep the anger up to prevent feeling shame or remorse about my actions.

During my angry period, I was always getting angry, but trying hard not to lash out. It was really unpleasant. Deciding I did not want to live in anger, I did some in-depth reading about the source of anger. What I found was that it was similar to addictive cravings, in that I could not control the arising of anger, but I could affect what happened after that. As it turns out, once anger has arisen, it will just go out unless it is given fuel. The fuel for anger is thoughts, like I described above, that keep me fixed on the injustice of the incident. It takes some practice to stop feeding anger, but it works.

My study of anger led to knowledge about how I propagated anger and how I could end it. Anger is a dubious luxury of greater people than me. This knowledge led me to practice *not* feeding my anger with a story when it arose. If there was something I could do about a situation, I would take action. If there was nothing I could do about the situation, I trained myself to let it go. This practice in turn led to the reduction in the length of time I was angry and the reduction in the incidences where anger arose. I do not yet have a complete cessation of anger, but I have 'realized' a significant reduction in anger and an elimination of angry behavior that I regret.

Now I take refuge in that realization and cessation. This is taking refuge in the dharma. It is taking refuge in the result of my spiritual practice. Not only can I rely on my realization to prevent me from doing angry behavior I subsequently have to "clean up", I can rely on it to know that I have the resources to change fixed and persistent behaviors. The realization of "ending" my anger provides me with a refuge when I have doubt about being able to change other obstinate maladaptive behaviors.

Other common realizations or cessations I hear people talk about experiencing as a result of their practice include freedom from addictive cravings, intolerance of abusive behavior, realization of greater sense of self, increase acceptance of the world, etc. All of these are possible places of refuge. You can take refuge in your own realization of them or the fact that they have been realized in others and therefore can be realized by you.

The other aspect of the Dharma Jewel is the path itself. For our purposes, this would be the Twelve Steps as presented in this work. Other paths are possible. The Buddha, in his first teaching, also mentioned the Aryan (or Noble) Eightfold Path as a way to achieve enlightenment. While the Third Noble Truth is the realization that suffering can be stopped, the Fourth Noble Truth explains how:

> This is the Noble Truth of the path leading to the cessation of suffering. It is simply the Aryan Eightfold Path, namely: right understanding, right thought, right speech, right action, right livelihood, right effort, right awareness, and right concentration.

The Buddha spent the rest of his life teaching students diverse in motivation and capacity how to develop the eight aspects of the path. Right speech, right action, and right livelihood refer to behaving in an ethical manner. These aspects of the Eightfold Path can be found in the Twelve Steps as steps Four through Ten and Step Twelve. The development of meditative concentration encompasses right effort, right awareness and right concentration. These are reflected in our Eleventh Step. The ideas of right understanding and right thought refer to the development of wisdom. Wisdom in the Twelve Steps is gained by completing steps One, Two, Three, Five, and Eleven.

Lam Rim – The Steps on the Path to Enlightenment

Tibetan Buddhists have a number of texts that describe the steps on the path to enlightenment. Indeed, many great Buddhist scholars have sought to organize the Buddha's teachings so that students can easily appreciate where a teaching fits into the overall map of enlightenment. These scholarly works are lam rims (steps on the path to enlightenment). While the Eightfold Path gives all the ingredients to reaching the human potential, the different aspects of the Eightfold Path are not meant to be developed sequentially, they are to be cultivated simultaneously.

> **Renunciation** is letting go of all things that do not support achieving our spiritual goals.

A lam rim, on the other hand, is typically presented in a manner that is followed sequentially. Although Lam Rims can be thousands of pages in length, they can also be brief. On the following pages is a short Lam Rim written by Je Tsongkapa (1357-1419). It takes us through the following steps:

STEPS OF LAM RIM	12 STEP CORRELATES
• Finding a spiritual teacher	• Finding a 12 Step Fellowship
• Gaining renunciation by realizing that life is short and worldly goals ultimately bring pain	• Turning our will and life over (Step 3) as a result of taking Step 1 and Step 2
• Cultivation of greater awareness and recollection	• Step 10 and Step 11
• Development of an ethical approach to life	• Taking personal inventory and clearing old karma – Step 4 to Step 10
• Development of bodhichitta	• Step 8
• Development of meditative concentration	• Step 11
• Development of wisdom (insight)	• Step 11
• Initiation into the secret teachings of Buddhism (the Diamond Way)	• Step 12 – as we progress on the spiritual path the essence of the secret teachings will be revealed to us naturally
• Completing the critical steps of the secret teachings	

This lam rim ends with a prayer for blessings and for quickening of the enlightenment process.

The Mandala of the Steps to Enlightenment (Lam Rim)
Je Tsongkapa Lobsang Drakpa 1357-1419

The source of all my good is my kind Lama, my Lord.

Bless me first to see that taking myself to him, in the proper way, is the very root of the path, and grant me then to serve and follow him with all my strength and reverence.

Bless me first to realize that the excellent life of leisure I have found, just this once, is ever so hard to find and ever so valuable;

Grant me then to wish, and never stop to wish, that I could take its essence night and day.

My body and the life in it are fleeting as the bubbles in the sea froth of a wave.

Bless me first thus to recall the death that will destroy me soon; And help me find sure knowledge that after I have died the things I've done, the white or black, and what these deeds will bring to me, follow always close behind, as certain as my shadow.

Grant me then ever to be careful, to stop the slightest wrongs of many wrongs we do, and try to carry out instead each and every good of the many that we may.

Bless me to perceive all that's wrong with the seemingly good things of this life. I can never get enough of them. They cannot be trusted. They are the door to every pain I have.

Grant me then to strive instead for the happiness of freedom.

Grant that these pure thoughts may lead me to be watchful and to recall what I should be doing.

Grant me to give the greatest care to make the vows of morality the essence of my practice; They are the root of the Buddha's teaching.

I have slipped and fallen into the sea of this suffering life; Bless me to see that every living being, every one my own mother, has fallen in too.

Grant me then to practice this highest wish for enlightenment, to take on myself the task of freeing them all.

Bless me to see clearly that the Wish itself is not enough, for if I am not well trained in the three moralities, I cannot become a Buddha.

Grant me then a fierce resolve to master the vows for children of the Victors.

Grant that I may quickly gain the path where quietude and insight join together; One which quiets my mind from being distracted to wrong objects. The other which analyzes the perfect meaning in the correct way.

Grant that once I have practiced well the paths shared and become a vessel that is worthy, I enter with perfect ease The Way of the Diamond, highest of all ways, holiest door to come inside for the fortunate and the good.

Bless me to know with genuine certainty that when I have entered thus, the cause that gives me both the attainments is keeping my pledges and vows most pure.

Grant me then to always keep them even if it costs my life.

Bless me next to realize precisely the crucial points of both the stages, the essence of the secret ways.

Grant me then to practice as the Holy One has spoken, putting all my effort in and never leaving off The Practice of the Four Times, highest that there is.

Bless me, grant me that the spiritual Guide who shows me this good road, and all my true companions in this quest live long and fruitful lives.

Bless and grant me that the rain of obstacles, things within me or outside me that could stop me now, stop and end forever.

In all my lives may I never live apart from my perfect Lamas, may I bask in the glory of the Dharma.

May I fulfill perfectly every good quality of every level and path, and reach then quickly the place where I become myself the Keeper of the Diamond.

Importance of a Clear Guide

Having a road map to reach spiritual goals is vital. The Twelve Steps provides such a road map. Taking refuge in the Steps themselves is much like turning to an instruction manual when you get a new piece of electronics to learn how to get it to work. It really is that simple. You put your faith in these instructions in order to be able to help you achieve your aspirations.

The refuge I most rely on is the Twelve Steps themselves. This is taking refuge in the Dharma Jewel. Whenever I have a persistent problem I work the Steps on it. The process either relieves me of unfounded stress or it provides me with the insight to know the next right action to take. My faith is based on witnessing countless others grow and find happiness using the Steps. It is strengthened by my own experience with the Steps.

Before I started using the Steps, I would read self-help books and find myself able to identify the problem, but unable to figure out exactly what to do or what instruction to apply to my situation. I think this is a common problem. For instance if someone hurts me do I "turn the other cheek"? Or do I "take care of myself assertively but with respect for others"?

In Buddhism, we are advised to not get beyond our current capacity. However, teachings usually lack any description or warning about who has the capacity to do a certain practice and who does not. I think it is expected that we would be under the guidance of a teacher, but today, the teachers are few and far between with little time to advise us in our day to day affairs. In program, the Steps offer guidance and the fellowship provides us with the support we need in determining what our capacity is. I take refuge in the Steps because they help me. When other practices fail, I can turn back to the Steps and get immediate clarity and serenity.

The Ultimate Form of the Three Jewels

The ultimate form of each of the Jewels refers to emptiness. An understanding of emptiness or a direct experience of emptiness is the ultimate refuge. It is the only thing that can really help us.

Emptiness is a simple, yet easy to misunderstand, concept. It is sometimes referred to as ultimate reality, since it describes the true way things exist. A complete understanding of it gives one the power to end all suffering. This is why it is considered the ultimate refuge.

Emptiness is a negative thing. It is the simple *absence* of independent existence. We touched on this concept in Step One when we discovered that there was not an "inherently suffering thing". A more elaborate presentation of emptiness can be found in Step Six. To explain it briefly we will use a simple example developed by Geshe Michael Roach involving a pen, a human and a dog.

Consider a pen. Does a pen exist as a "pen", meaning something that one writes with? The answer is no. If a dog sees me waving a pen around, he does not recognize it as something to write with, but something to chase or chew. He sees the object I consider a "pen" and instead recognizes it as a "chew toy".

Just as we cannot find a thing that is considered universally "bad" to all people, we cannot find a "pen" that exists. Of course I am not suggesting that pens do not exist conventionally. They exist conventionally and they work just fine. But if a pen existed ultimately as a pen (something to write with) then even a dog would recognize it as a pen and would not dream of chewing on it.

So what causes me to see a cylindrical object and think "pen" while a dog sees the same object and thinks "chew toy"? That would be my karma. Indeed, it could be claimed that the difference between a dog and a human is the karma to see a cylinder as a chew toy instead of a pen.

What we see is dependent on our personal karma. And our karma is dependent on our thoughts and actions. It is within the marriage of karma and emptiness that we find the key to freedom. Because the things around us are empty we can create the causes and conditions (karma) that will force us to see the world free of suffering, aging and death. When we take refuge in emptiness we are taking refuge in an understanding of how things really work. Understanding how things really work and orchestrating our life to be in alignment with this is the only way to get protection from what we would like to avoid.

When we begin to see a world free of suffering, is the world really changing or are we just making it up?

The fact that things are empty does not mean that we can "imagine" they are something else. Sometimes in Buddhism conventional reality is referred to as an illusion. Yes, it is an illusion in the sense that everything seems to be self-existent, but that does not mean that it is in an illusion like a dream or mirage. Non-self existent knives still cut and can kill. The only way to change the "illusion" that functions like real is by changing our thoughts and actions. When we change our karma the world does change. It does become free of suffering just as truly as our current world is full of suffering. This is not a "reframing" process.

Emptiness is our ultimate refuge. It manifests in the Three Jewels as:

- the emptiness of a Buddha

- the realizations of emptiness and the teachings (or path) that lead to an understanding of emptiness (Dharma)

- any person that has perceived emptiness directly (Sangha).

Other refuges are possible such as relying on a sponsor or teacher, but it is always best to consider why they are useful. That is, consider the emptiness of the situation and what is really going on from an emptiness perspective.

For example, when I have a headache I take refuge in ibuprofen. Does ibuprofen cure headaches? No, if there was some part of ibuprofen that could relieve headaches then it would always relieve headaches for me and for everyone, and it does not. So why do I turn to ibuprofen for relief? I have an understanding of the emptiness of the headache and of ibuprofen. I understand that my headache is a result of past thoughts and actions. I also realize that for ibuprofen to work, I must also have the karma for the headache to go away. My action to take ibuprofen is based on a belief that it can help me (that belief is also a result of my karma). I believe that it is my intention to get relief that allows for the ripening of the karma to have my headache go away. In addition, it seems that the more belief I have in the object I go to for refuge, the better the results I get.

The apparent refuge we take will vary depending on the situation. As we work through the Steps and evaluate our results, we will find the best refuge for us. What we turn to for protection and aid may change, grow, and evolve and most certainly will have an aspect that is personal. Frequently our relationship with our refuge may be hard to describe or explain.

Completing Step Three

We complete Step Three when we decide to give the spiritual principles embodied in the Twelve Steps a try. Surrendering our will and lives means we give up our old, ineffective ways and attempt to align our will and lives with the insights we gain by working the Twelve Steps. We begin to see the emptiness of the world around us, including what we think of as our own self.

Sometimes Step Three is considered a step where we surrender. If this was the case it would read, "We surrender our will and lives..." In this step, we make a decision to surrender. The remaining steps teach us how and give us faith born of tangible results to accomplish this.

The process of taking Step Three is like making a decision to run a marathon. For most of us that does not mean we will be able to go out the next day and do it. It simply means that we are planning on doing it. That decision then shapes our next actions. In order to run a marathon we will need to undertake certain training steps. The decision starts us on the path.

People that are reading the literature, coming to meetings, sharing, talking with other program members, or working the Steps have all completed Step Three. Since they are using the program, they must have made a decision to give it a try. This demonstrates enough faith to get started. Moving to do Step Four is confirmation that the decision has been made and the Third Step is completed.

List of all desires

Thought & feeling, memory

Date (time / location ⇒) Thoughts Feelings

STEP FOUR
Made a searching and fearless moral inventory of ourselves.

The rationale for taking the Fourth Step is given in the Big Book of Alcoholics Anonymous. The authors claim that our problem is a symptom and that we have to get down to the causes and conditions. This is accomplished with a personal inventory aimed at uncovering the flaws in our make-up.

How true it is that our problems are the result of causes and conditions. In essence, this has been the take-home message of the first three steps. However, the perspective of a Buddhist regarding the cause of our character is different from the traditional view. We are seeking to have a transformation of our person, just like the founders of the Twelve Step movement; but in contrast we believe that our defects are not under the control of a creator being who somehow gave us these flaws and under sincere appeal (Step Seven) will remove them from us.

If not God, what is the creator of our world and of ourselves?

We find the answer in the first line of the fourth chapter of the *Abhidharmakosa*:[3]

Karmic deeds cause the multitude of worlds.

---

[3] The **Abhidharmakosa** (Treasure house of knowledge), a book that is widely respected by many schools of Mahayana Buddhism, was written by **Master Vasubhandu** (~350AD). This book contains the Abhidharma school's tenets organized in eight chapters: (1) Categories of Existence , (2) Sense Powers, (3) The Suffering World, (4) Karma, (5) How Bad Thoughts Motivate, (6) How to Escape Suffering, (7) Wisdom, and (8) Balanced Meditation.

This simple statement has profound ramifications. It suggests that the world we see and experience, from a leaf on a tree to the emotion of contentment we feel, is created by what we have done in the past. No detail is too small to not have been created by our past deeds. The bacteria in our gut and the planets in other galaxies fall under the domain of our karma. Simply incredible!

Our personality is similarly shaped by our past. If you have a tendency to lie, that tendency is created by lying in the past. If you have a tendency to be generous, that is likewise a trait that is caused by past thoughts and actions. The personality you were born with could be much more challenging to live with than other peoples' personalities. We are not born "equal". Some of us have it harder than others. We are powerless in any one moment over our character traits, but we are not powerless over taking action to change them.

These ideas make more sense to me than the possibility that our character was the creation of some being. Why would a creator give me the tendency to have compulsive addictions unless they wanted to punish me or perhaps enjoyed giving me trouble? It seems just as much an injustice that I was born with addictive tendencies as it is I was born with the positive tendency to tell the truth that others do not possess. My life is not better than some because God likes me or worse than others because they are his favorites.

When I consider that we are all struggling under limitations that are imposed on us by actions done in the past which we cannot even remember, I feel great compassion – both for myself and others. The bottom line is that our current situation is not really our fault, in the sense that we did not know how things worked up until now. However, now that we do know how things work, we can create a different future – one that can begin blossoming immediately.

The reason we take a searching and fearless moral inventory is to facilitate cleaning up the past so that it will not come back to hurt us. In Buddhism, what we do creates our future. While there are ethical guidelines, there is no "good" or "bad".

The criteria for evaluating our actions is simple. If we have done things in the past that we would not want to happen to us, then we will need to undertake some corrective action. The method the Buddha taught is called the Four Powers

> **Inventory Tip**
> There is no absolute "good" or "bad". The criteria for evaluating our actions is simple. If what we have done we would not want done to us, then we note this action (or thought) on our inventory.

and is discussed in detail in Step Ten. If our past actions give us reason to smile, then we can expect pleasant results arising from those actions and will want to rejoice. Further, rejoicing over the positive things we have thought and done will facilitate the results of those deeds manifesting in our life faster.

Karmic Gardening

A review of how we create our world will allow us to undertake the work of the Fourth Step with our purpose clearly in mind. The workings of karma are much too complex for me to know, but the model I like to use explains karma as follows: When we do or think anything, our mind witnesses this act and an impression is made in the mind. The capacity of the mind is infinite and everything we do could easily be recorded there. As a gardener, I like to think of these impressions as seeds.

For example, let's say I give a dollar to a hungry and homeless person on the street. In general, when I do anything my mind records everything about the act: my generosity, my motive (Did I think I could get something in return?), the value of the object being given (Was it something I needed myself?), the state of the recipient (Were they in need of the thing I gave?). All aspects of the act are recorded in my mind.

What happens next is that the "seed" just hangs out as a mental potential. As it incubates it also tends to grow. That is just one of the aspects of karmic seeds. The result of a karma is always greater than the cause. Just like an oak tree is much bigger than the acorn it originates from. At some point, the seed ripens and the result of my action is experienced. My world is at that moment "created" by the earlier action. In this example, my dollar might come back to me as a 100-dollar gift or perhaps a raise at work. The seed created by giving can either ripen as receiving or as the habit to give more. This is because the original seed was created when we saw someone (ourselves) give and saw a second person receive. When it ripens we experience an event that is similar in context to the original event but not necessarily identical.

If we haphazardly do good things, we will haphazardly experience good things in our life. Positive will always bring us positive. This would be like throwing a bunch of good seed on the ground and then letting nature take its course. There is a good chance that some of the seeds will germinate and produce a crop.

On the other hand, if we select our seeds carefully, plant the tomatoes in the sun and the mint in the shade, and then care for the garden (the garden being analogous to our mindstream) with water and fertilizer (positive thoughts, intentions, and deeds) we will find that our harvest will be greater and predictable. (We will get tomatoes and mint – and lots of them!)

We can use the same approach to cultivate "karma". If I give the person on the street a dollar, understanding karma and holding the intention that it comes back to me in the form of greater income, I will find that my income increases and not that someone throws me a birthday party, which would be another form of receiving. I can use my intention to direct the growth of karmic seeds.

It might seem that this is a blatantly selfish approach. The giving is directly connected to getting something in return. However, it is simply "intelligent self-interest". It is impossible to escape the pleasant results of doing a positive action. Why not use the opportunity to guide those pleasant results in a direction that also fulfills a concrete need or desire? Indeed, as we will see later the attitude of the mind also influences what karma ripens when. Giving naturally invokes good feelings. This is further accentuated by the knowledge that in addition to helping another person you have also directly helped yourself.

There are other ways to potentiate the results of actions. With any action there is the object of the action (this would be the person or institution that experience the action) and there is the object itself. There is a hierarchy of value in both the receiver and the object. (See the potency chart on the next page.) If I am giving my last dollar or a portion of my money that I would rather spend on myself, it is considered of greater value than if I am giving something of no value to me or my surplus money. Similarly, giving when I except a material return (tax credit or free gift) is of lesser value than giving with no return.

The hierarchy for the recipient of giving follows this pattern. In general, the best objects are ones that can reduce the suffering for the greatest number of living beings. This puts a human before an animal (since humans are closer to enlightenment – a state where they can help more beings). A person in need or that is sick or suffering is of higher value than someone that is not. A group of people would come before an individual. In addition, fairly high objects include: people or institutions that are in the position to help groups of suffering/needy people; beings that have done you a prior kindness such as your parents (giving you a precious human life); teachers or mentors; and spiritual leaders or organizations.

A negative deed is potentiated in the same way. Hurting our parents or someone that has helped us is worse than hurting a stranger. Hurting someone intentionally is worse than hurting someone accidentally. Killing a human is worse than killing a mosquito. Stealing from someone that is suffering and needy would be worse than stealing the surplus from the rich. All these actions plant seeds that will result in ourselves being hurt, killed, or robbed, but to different extremes.

Now that we have looked at the nature of karmic seeds, let's consider the garden, or environment, that they ripen in as another aspect of how we can affect our future. As I have mentioned before, if we have had countless past lives, there is a good chance that we have the potential propagating in our mindstream for any possible future. I purport that what grows is under our control to some extent.

Potency Chart

Recipients of Our Actions
- Enlightened Beings
- People in position to help many people (spiritual organization or institutions)
- Spiritual teachers, mentors, guides
- Biological Parents
- Someone that has helped you (potency depends on level of help received)
- Suffering or needy groups of people
- Groups of people
- Suffering or needy individuals
- Humans
- Animals

Objects for Our Actions
- Something I need myself
- Something I think is valuable
- Extra stuff I have
- Something that I don't value

Attitude During Our Actions
- Acting with passion or devotion (either great love or great hate)
- Acting with moderate emotion
- Acting without thought or care

Increasing Potency

My "natural" tendency is to be melancholy, pessimistic, and critical. If the environment of my mind is dominated by these attitudes, the seeds that ripen will tend to foster this same attitude and the world I see will always be disappointing. If I want to see a world that is growing, blossoming, and unified, I need to add different fertilizer. This is the place where I have to adopt a practice of replacing my attitude of "my cup being half empty" with one where I entertain thoughts that focus on the good I see. In program, we call this "acting as if". I act as if the world is the way I want it to be. The practice of changing the mental environment that the karmic seeds abide in takes diligence, but even small efforts are rewarded because the karma of making the effort results in it being easier to make the effort in the future.

One other thing that can aide in creating a more fertile mindstream is being part of groups that are positive and growth-oriented. This is one of the prime benefits of Twelve Step fellowship meetings. If I am not able to clear my mind of repetitive negative thoughts, getting myself into an environment where the messages are positive will naturally foster a shift in my own mental pattern. This is another reason many people in program find it advantageous to remove themselves from negative relationships or at least distance themselves from situations that foster the behaviors and attitudes they would like to be free of.

The Inventory

Many fellowships offer tools for making a searching and fearless moral inventory. They are all very good and useful. I have included a list of questions based on the Ten Misdeeds at the end of this chapter. My intention is not to try to improve on the other methods available, but just to offer another option. The method you use to take your inventory does not matter. Just pick the one you are attracted to at this moment and quickly complete it.

Only a fragment of the impulses that drive us are conscious to the mind. You will find that as you change and grow more will be revealed. These revelations can become the material for future Fourth Steps (or Tenth Steps).

I have worked my way through the Steps many times and usually use a different method for taking the Fourth Step each time. The key is to inventory the events that stick out in our minds. We do not need some outside authority to tell us what is right or wrong. Our gut and heart will lead the way. I have found that over the years my ethical barometer has changed. For instance, I used to think nothing of driving six or seven miles-an-hour above the speed limit. Now, I drive at the speed limit, simply because I understand who made the law. Further, I want to "see" other people respecting my rules. (Actually, I have taken to driving under the speed limit now; it is amazing how much gasoline I save!)

Ways to help us get started with our inventory abound. The *Alcoholics Anonymous Big Book* offers the nice suggestion of considering the people or institutions we are resentful of (Fourth edition, page 64). Alternately, one can go through one's life chronologically. Frequently, specific behaviors dominate certain relationships or time periods and the Fourth Step can be organized around these. Tony A., the founder of Adult Children of Alcoholics, suggests we "inventory our parents because, in essence, we had become them". Now there is a novel idea! Certainly the lists of questions published by many Twelve Step fellowships are extremely useful inventory tools. For instance, Al-Anon has a comprehensive and quite daunting guide called *Blueprint for Progress*.

The Buddha recognized over 80,000 misdeeds that are summarized in a list of the top ten. I cringe to use the word misdeed, since the "misdeeds" are not about right and wrong. They are misdeeds in the sense that most people would not want to experience being the recipient of the action. In that sense, they are deeds to avoid doing.

Here is the list of the top ten. They are not the top ten because they are the worst, but simply because they are the ones we do on a daily basis. Since we do them all the time, we are most apt to experience the fruit of these coming back into our lives in the form of having them done to us. The list is typically grouped by what is called the "doors of expression". The three doors of expression are: physical action, verbal action, and mental action.

Ten Misdeeds

Physical Action

1) Killing
2) Stealing (Taking anything of value that was not given.)
3) Sexual Misconduct (mainly adultery or sexual behavior that hurts others)

Verbal Action

4) Lying
5) Harsh Words
6) Divisive Talk (speech meant to split people apart)
7) Idle Chatter

Mental Action

8) Coveting
9) Ill Will
10) Wrong World View (disbelief in karma and emptiness)

A Fourth Step could be organized around the Ten Misdeeds as well. If you are considering this, some useful questions and considerations can be found at the end of this chapter. When using this list to guide our inventory, it is useful to consider how close we have ever come to committing a misdeed as well as in what situations have we upheld the converse action as summarized in the following list:

Reciprocals of the Ten Misdeeds: The Ten Virtues

Physical Action
1) Protecting life
2) Giving
3) Respectful Sexual Conduct (helping people stay together)

Verbal Action
4) Telling the Truth
5) Kind Words
6) Supportive Talk (speech meant to keep people together)
7) Appropriate Silence or Meaningful Talk

Mental Action
8) Non-Attachment and Well-Wishing
9) Rejoicing
10) Correct World View (understanding karma and emptiness)

My understanding is that when the fellowship of Alcoholic Anonymous started, the Steps were worked quickly – in a matter of hours or perhaps a couple days. This makes a lot of sense to me. If you have a life-threatening disease, do you complete the treatment as soon as possible or do you delay until you are sure you can do it perfectly? I recommend going through the Steps quickly the first time and then immediately starting them again if you desire to study them more thoroughly.

Indeed, at the beginning, before the Steps were written down and formalized, the key step was Step Twelve. The founder stories all focus on reaching out to help a fellow sufferer. This was considered the key to sobriety. The early members would go searching for others to help.

From a Buddhist perspective based on karma – the only way to stay sober would be to help someone else stay sober. Unless we have the seed for helping others get what they want, we will not be able to achieve our own goals. This is a primary incentive to move through the Steps quickly the first time.

The Four Powers: Clearing Old Negative Karma

Ten minutes in my head reveals that on a typical day I am more apt to have thoughts that are pessimistic, jealous, suspicious, and aimed at protecting myself from possible threats than I am to have purely positive thoughts. I might think subtle negative things like, "I wish I had the health, partner, etc. of that other person," or maybe, "Can I trust this person?" Or I might have more blatant thoughts that arise like, "Good! That driver deserved to get a ticket," or "I wish they would have a fight and break up so I could be with him more." As I grow I still have these thoughts pop up spontaneously, although now I counter them as best I can with a conscious opposite thought.

The Buddha recognized that it would be easy to consider spiritual development impossible since we are constantly piling up negative karma in the form of thoughts and deeds. He explained in the sutra entitled *The Teaching of the Four Practices* how negative karmic seeds can be prevented from ripening. The four forces used to purify negative karma are:

- Foundation Power
- Power of Destruction
- Power of Restraint
- Power of the Antidote

The four forces will be considered in detail in Step Ten where we explore the process of taking a continuous inventory of our thoughts and behavior. These same four forces form the foundation of the spiritual principles embodied in steps Three through Ten. Step Three gives us the foundation power. Step Four and Step Five give us the power of destruction. Step Six and Step Seven give us the power of restraint and steps Six through Nine give us the power of the antidote. Step Ten utilizes all Four Powers. Rest assured that while negative karma cannot be lost once it is completed, it can be destroyed – just like a seed can be prevented from germinating if put in a inhospitable climate.

Completing Step Four

We have completed Step Four when we have in hand a written inventory of our actions and thoughts based on the method we chose to use. Most people find it useful to not only catalog the events that were negative, but also include an inventory of positive actions and thoughts. A balanced inventory is advantageous for effective karmic gardening. Rejoicing over the positive things we have done will attract the fruits of those actions to us quicker. We move on to Step Five confident that by working the remaining steps we can destroy the seeds we have planted that we do not want coming back to us.

Inventory Questions

Killing/Protecting Life

Have I killed anyone? Have I helped kill anyone?

Have I killed animals or other living beings?

How close have I come to killing?

Have I hit or hurt anyone physically?

Have I saved someone's life?

How do I act to protect life?

Have I acted to make an environment safe by removing obstacles in a path or by other means?

Have I prevented people from harming themselves or others?

Stealing/Giving

Have I robbed anyone or a business?

Have I used my employer's resources by making personal copies at work or taking office supplies home from work?

Have I "stolen" people's time by leaving a mess they had to clean up or by meaningless talk?

When have I given or been generous with my possessions, my money and my time?

Sexual Misconduct/Respectful Sexual Conduct

Have I had sex with another person's partner? (Perhaps when one of the "partners" felt broken up, but the other considered them in a relationship still?)

Have I forced or coerced someone to have sexual contact with me?

Have I cheated on my partner?

Have I tried to split people up that are in relationship with each other?

Have I refrained from flirting with someone I was attracted to that was in a committed relationship?

Have I done things sexually that I felt were not right?

Have I used restraint to avoid sexual behaviors I was drawn to, but did not feel right about doing?

Can I look upon my sexual conduct with satisfaction?

Lying/Telling the Truth

Have I lied? What about 'white' lies?

Have I mislead someone?

Have I refrained from speaking to avoid telling the truth?

Have I deceived someone in other ways?

Do I tend to be honest?

Am I honest even when it may result in unpleasantness?

Have I denied something to myself or others that was really true?

Do I hide parts of myself?

Have I withheld information that would have benefitted another?

Am I straightforward in my communication?

Harsh Words/Kind Words

Have I called people names, put them down or spoken with the intent to hurt them?

Have I yelled at people?

Have I made noise that disturbed others?

Have I been "brutally" honest when it was unnecessary?

Have I been critical and controlling?

Have I praised or complemented people?

Do I let people know they are appreciated and liked?

Have I created beautiful sounds that people enjoy?

Divisive Talk/ Supportive Speech

Have I talked about people behind their backs? Have I gossiped?

Have I spoken ill about anyone, even if deserved? (Including political figures or leaders that I do not agree with.)

Have I tried to break groups or communities up?

Have I said things that have undermined individuals or groups?

Do I praise people to others?

Have I worked to create harmony and cohesion in groups?

Have I worked to inspire and uplift people?

Have I encouraged others to follow their heart?

Have I worked to bring people together in community?

Idle Chatter/ Meaningful Talk

Have I chattered on about topics without a purpose such as to inform action or uplift the listener?

Have I complained about something incessantly?

Do I repeat news that really has no meaning in my life or the lives of others?

Do I waste people's time by rehashing the same thing over and over again?

Have I spoken out to warn someone of danger or a threat?

Do I remain silent when I have nothing of importance to say?

Have I shared spiritual messages or taught people how the program works?

Have I helped people learn something that will benefit them?

Do I talk about things only with a purpose to inform action or uplift the listener?

Do I consider my motive for speaking?

Do I have a purpose for the things I say?

One of the program slogans is THINK (before you speak), meaning: is what you are going to say Thoughtful, Honest, Intelligent, Necessary, and Kind. This is a good rule of thumb for evaluating "right" speech.

Coveting/Non-attachment and Well-wishing

Have I spent lots of time wishing I had things or characteristics I do not?

Have I wished I had things that people I know have?

Have I thought about dishonest or immoral ways to get the things that others have that I want?

Have I resented the attention that others get?

Have I had strong cravings for certain things? (like my drug of choice)

Have I worked to stop cravings for what others have?

Have I worked to stop cravings for excess things?

Do I appreciate what I have?

Am I able to accept when something I like is lost or broken?

Have I been genuinely happy when someone has something I want but do not have myself?

Ill will/Rejoicing

Have I been happy when someone I do not like has something bad happen to them?

Have I hoped that harm would come to people I do not like?

Do I think people deserve the bad that happens to them?

Have I rejoiced when something good happens to someone, even if I do not like the person or I had wanted the good to happen to me?

Am I happy when people get what they want?

Do I want everyone to be happy?

Wrong Views/Correct View

Do I think that if I do something wrong and do not get caught, it is okay?

Do I believe, one hundred percent, that when my body dies the mind does not go on.

Do I believe there are no consequences to my actions? That the law of karma is one hundred percent wrong?

Do I believe that I can create a more pleasant future by acting kind and compassionate now?

STEP FIVE
Admitted to all that is, to ourselves, and to another human being the exact nature of our actions.

The Exact Nature of Our Actions

Once we have completed the inventory of our past in Step Four, we move to Step Five, where we investigate the motivations behind the actions and patterns we uncovered in our inventory. In this step, we are called upon to determine the "exact nature" of our actions and then admit to them. In addition, we tell them to another human being. This act of "admitting" is the foundational force behind the power of destruction of negative karma. In Step Four, we cultivated a sense of intelligent remorse based on an understanding that some of our actions could lead us to additional suffering in the short- or long-term future. In Step Five, we formally admit what we did, and, more importantly, the driving force behind the action.

In our Fourth Step inventory, we may have encountered, for instance, a tendency to tell lies. Here, in Step Five, we ask ourselves, "Why?" We may find that sometimes we lied to people to avoid their disapproval or disappointment. In such circumstances, perhaps we have the habit of "people-pleasing". Other times we may have lied in an attempt to avoid punishment. Sometimes we may have exaggerated to make ourselves look good or to gain extra attention. There might also have been circumstances where we had no reason to tell a falsehood, yet did so because it was a habit or it just made conversation more interesting.

Investigating the situations when we lied a little deeper, we may find that the majority of time we tell a lie we are motivated by fear. This may either be a fear of conflict and punishment or fear that somehow we are not enough as we are. We may, on some level, have thought that we would not get the material things we needed or our emotional or physical needs met unless we lied. If we lied casually, it may be that we did not have any

55

good reason to stop. We may have simply never considered lying a problem up until now.

Fear is such a common underlying drive that in program the acronym FEAR (False Evidence Appearing Real) is commonly referred to. It is a reminder that whenever we encounter fear we have lost connection to our refuge or understanding of the way things ultimately are. Fear can only arise out of deceptive reality, a reality where it appears we can control things in the moment they arise. Fear is dispelled by the understanding of how things actually work.

In Step Five we learn that an incorrect world view is underneath the motivation to do any action that does not serve us. This means we fail to recognize, in the moment of our action, that our deed can only result in something similar happening to us. Consider lying. In the moment of our lie, we may entertain vague notions that our lying does not matter if we are not caught or that lying is the only way to have our needs met. We may also notice that sometimes when we lie, we get the result we are trying for. We forget, when we lie, our mind records the action and plants a seed or mental potential for lying. Unless destroyed by our conscious volition, that seed will ripen in the future and produce a similar result. What we experience based on our action can vary somewhat, but it must resemble the initial deed. If we told a lie, then we will be lied to, we may acquire the habit of lying or perhaps people will not believe us when we tell the truth.

The Possible Consequences of Our Actions

Je Tsongkapa (1357-1419) explains the correlations between specific non-virtues and their karmic results in his book *The Great Book on the Steps of the Path*. These correlations are presented next. I remind the reader that the workings of karma are considered very subtle and extremely difficult to follow in real time. Also, the Buddha instructs us not to believe anything blindly. So, take what you like and leave the rest.

I am presenting these correlations only because they can be useful in promoting behavior that is truly more self-serving. Since Step Five is all about what motivates us, it seems appropriate to give some time to the details of cause and effect as this knowledge can be quite motivating. Je Tsongkapa, the gentleman that passed these correlations on to us, is renowned for his ability to clarify and condense earlier teachings. He was a leader of the Gelugpa branch of Tibetan Buddhism. Further, he has received an important endorsement. His literary works have been praised by the 14th Dalai Lama as being profound and true to tradition.

All of our thoughts and actions are causes for specific results. If a deed is particularly horrendous, Tibetan Buddhism tells us we can expect the result to ripen into a rebirth in one of the lower realms. We may find ourselves in hell or living as a hungry ghost or animal. If we manage to come back as a human, then a negative action can lead to three types of results:

- the personal (or consistent) action consequence

- the personal (or consistent) experience consequence

- the environmental consequence

The **personal action consequence** is such that we will gain the habit to do the same type of deed over and over. For instance, if we engaged in gossip, the personal action consequence would be the tendency to gossip in the future. Whatever we do creates the predisposition to repeat this same behavior.

The personal action consequence is a powerful motivator for putting effort into cultivating positive habits. Initial investment of energy in creating a healthy habit will result in greater ease in repeating that healthy behavior in the future. This is simply part of the law of cause and effect (karma).

Consequences of Our Actions
Personal Action: We gain the habit to repeat the same action.
Personal Experience: We have the same type of thing happen to us that we did.
Environmental: Our surroundings reflect our past deeds.

The **personal experience consequences** are correlated to their misdeed in the following list:

1. Killing: Your life is short and you get sick easily.

2. Stealing: You do not have enough to live on and/or you have to share what you do have as common property with others.

3. Sexual Misconduct: The people who work around you are unreliable and you find yourself having a lot of competition for your partner.

4. Lying: No one believes what you say, even when you are speaking the truth and others are always deceiving you.

5. Harsh Words: You hear many unpleasant things and when others talk to you it always seems to you as if they want to start a fight.

6. Divisive Talk: The people around you are always fighting against one another and you are surrounded by undesirable characters.

7. Idle Chatter: No one respects what you say—no one thinks that what you say has any particular value, and you are afflicted with a lack of confidence.

8. Coveting: Your personality is dominated by desire and you are never satisfied with what you have.

9. Ill Will: You are always finding yourself without help or are unable to get the help you need. You are always hurting others or always being hurt by others.

10. Wrong World View: You become a person who keeps harmful views or are deceitful person.

Although Je Tsongkapa did not give the reciprocals, we can easily imagine what they would be. I would recommend focusing on the reciprocals as a way to attract these positive circumstances into your life. This is a potent way to do "karmic gardening".

1. Protecting Life: Your life is long and you stay healthy or heal quickly.

2. Giving: You have more than enough to live on and extra to share.

3. Respectful Sexual Conduct: The people who work around you are reliable and you find yourself with a devoted partner. Everyone respects and honors your relationship.

4. Telling the Truth: You are believed. People always tell you the truth.

5. Kind Words: You hear many pleasant things and when others talk to you they are always positive.

6. Supportive Talk: The people around you get along well. You are surrounded by people of the highest character.

7. Appropriate Silence or Meaningful Talk: People respect what you say and they think what you have to say is valuable. You have a good self esteem.

8. Non-Attachment and Well-Wishing: You are satisfied with what you have.

9. Rejoicing: People are always offering you help and you have no needs. People appreciate your kindness and they are kind to you.

10. Correct World View: You are a truthful and wise person. You know how to respond most effectively in all circumstances.

The **environmental consequences** explain the physical environment we live in based on the karmic cause. These are quite interesting.

1. The consequence of killing expresses itself in the outer world around you. Food, drink, medicine, the crops in the fields, and other such things have very little power; they are always inferior; they have little nutrition or potency; they are hard to digest, and they cause disease in you. Because of this the majority of the living beings around you die before reaching the end of a full life.

2. Because you have stolen, then the crops are few and far between; the crops have no power to remove hunger; they spoil; they never come up; dry spells stay on too long; it rains too much; the crops dry up, or die off.

3. Because you have done sexual misconduct, you live in a place where there is urine and feces all around, and mud and dirt and filth, and everything stinks, and everywhere seems unpleasant and distasteful.

4. Because you have lied, you live in a world where, when you undertake farming or some work in cooperation with other people, in the end the work fails to prosper, and the people cannot work well together, and for the most part everyone is cheating one another, and is afraid, and where there are many things to be afraid of.

5. Because you have split people up with your talk, the very ground in the place you live is all uneven, covered with crags and gullies, full of highs and lows, so that you can travel only with difficulty, and where you are always afraid, and there are many things to be afraid of.

6. Because you have spoken harsh words, the ground where you live is covered with obstacles like the trunks of fallen trees, and thorns, and stones, and clods of dirt, and lots of sharp broken pieces of glass; it's rough and dreary; no streams, or lakes, or springs of water; the whole earth is parched, poisoned with salt and borax, burning hot, useless, threatening; a place where there are many things to fear.

7. Because you have talked meaninglessly, fruits refuse to grow on the trees, or they start to grow at the wrong times, never at the right times, and seem ripe when they are still not ripe, or their roots are

frail, or they cannot stay long; there are no places to take your leisure, no parks, no glades, no pools of cool water, and many things around to make you afraid.

8. Because you have coveted what others have, then each and every good thing you ever manage to find starts to get worse and worse, less and less with the passing of each of the four seasons, and in every month, and even day by day.

9. Because you have wished bad things on others, you live in a world of chaos, where diseases spread, and evil is everywhere, and plague, and conflict, and fear from the armies of other nations; where there are many lions or leopards or other dangerous animals; where there are everywhere venomous snakes or scorpions or poison biting worms; surrounded by harmful spirits, and thieves or muggers, and the like.

10. Because you have held wrong views, then you live in a world where the single highest source of happiness is steadily disappearing from the earth; a world where people think that things that are unclean and things that are suffering are actually nice, and happy; a world where there is no place to go, no one to help, nothing to protect you.

Wow! Quite an order, no? I get some comfort by having my world so entirely explained. However, I am not sure how useful this information is on a practical level. We are advised to keep an open mind, but deciding if these correlations are true or not is not a priority for me. My personal method for adopting beliefs was discussed in Step Two. Based on my method, I cannot see any advantage to believing or disbelieving these correlations.

As it happens, I already do not want to lie, cheat, kill and steal because those actions make me feel bad and steal my peace of mind. That is enough for me. I am not concerned about the environment they also cause since my choice to avoid them is made based on a more tangible result. Still the list is interesting.

What do you think the reciprocals would be? Here is my list.

1. The consequence of protecting life expresses itself in the outer world around you. Food, drink, medicine, the crops in the fields, and other such things have great power; they are organic, very nutritious and potent. They are easy to digest and they create

health in you. Because of the fine quality of food and medicine the beings around you live long healthy lives.

2. Because you have practiced generosity, the crops are abundant; they nourish and satisfy; the harvest is plentiful and lasts long in storage; and the weather is conducive to perfect crop growth and harvest.

3. Because you have engaged in respectful sexual conduct, you live in a place that is beautiful, clean and pleasant smelling.

4. Because you have told the truth, you live in a world where your joint, cooperative efforts are successful and people work well together. You feel safe and there is nothing to be afraid of.

5. Because you have supported people with your talk, the land that you live on is even and smooth; it is easy to travel around. You feel safe and there is nothing to be afraid of.

6. Because you have spoken kind words, the ground where you live is clear of obstacles. It is pleasant and refreshing with streams, lakes and springs of water. There is nothing to be afraid of.

7. Because you have talked meaningfully, fruits grow on the trees and ripen at the right times; the trees have strong roots; there are many places to take your leisure: parks, glades, and pools of cool water. There is nothing to be afraid of.

8. Because you have practiced non-attachment to what others have, each and every good thing you get continues to grow and get better and better with the passing of the four seasons and in every month, and even day by day.

9. Because you have wished good things on others, you live in a world of harmony, where goodness and health abounds; where there are only creatures of peace and beauty.

10. Because you have held correct views, you live in a world where everyone appreciates and honors the single highest source of happiness; a world where people practice love, compassion and hold correct view. There are many places to go and many people that will help and guide you.

Sweet! The idea of being able to create a new world based on my actions is very nice. However, regardless of future outcomes, letting our actions be guided by the Ten Virtues is certainly a pleasant way to live – both for ourselves and everyone around us.

The Three Poisons – The Root of all Self-Defeating Actions

The Buddha described the basic motivations that keep us unhappy and suffering as "craving" and "aversion". These mental poisons can also be referred to as "ignorant liking" and "ignorant disliking". A third mental poison is ignorance itself. The "three poisons" can be found represented at the center of Wheel of Life pictures as a pigeon or rooster (ignorant liking) and a snake (ignorant disliking) coming forth from a pig's mouth (ignorance).

The three poisons work like this: Ignorance is the basic foundation. It is our tendency to view the world and the things in it as things we can control, manipulate and dominate. This belief is subtle and ignores the ideas of cause and effect. When we come in contact with things, they appear to us as pleasant or unpleasant and, based on our mistaken foundation view, we may want to keep the good things (or get rid of the bad things) so much that we lie, cheat, steal, kill, etc. to do so. If we are wise we understand our powerlessness over things in the moment. We still experience things as pleasant or unpleasant, but our

The Three Poisons
(1) Craving or ignorant liking
(2) Aversion or ignorant disliking
(3) Ignorance itself

liking and disliking do not result in thoughts and actions that will bring us grief in the future.

The difference between liking and ignorant liking is the world view behind them, the "pig" so to speak. In Buddhism, we are down on ignorant disliking and craving, but we are all for enjoying life and seeking pleasure in a balanced, conscious way. The real problem with ignorant disliking and liking is not the liking or disliking, but the "ignorant" part. It is due to our "ignorance" that we foolishly do things that we would not want done to us. The actions that are motivated by not understanding cause and effect and by having desire or aversion is what perpetuates our suffering.

For example, let's say we have been sexual with someone that is not our partner and we know that this will upset our partner. Because we do not want to lose our current partner, we deny our infidelity. Because we like having a partner, we tell our partner a lie. We think that lying will ensure that we keep our partner. However, lying can only result in people lying to *us* in the future. In our model, the fact that we have a partner is due to the fruition of the karmic seeds we planted in the past. We have a partner today because we respected other peoples' relationships in the past. In our ignorance, we believe that lying will ensure our partner stays with us. Liking our partner is okay, as is undertaking actions that nurture our relationship, but ignorant liking is a problem. Ignorant liking manifests in this situation as blindly doing a misdeed in an attempt to keep our partner.

Another aspect of ignorance can manifest as how we view our partner. We may see our partner as someone outside of ourselves that we can win or lose, when actually it is a wrong view to consider our partner as completely independent of us. The correct view is that our experience of a partner is completely dependent on our own karmic potentials and because of this, nothing we do in this moment can actually effect whether we have a partner or not. What is happening in our life is due to seeds that were planted earlier. We cannot do anything in the moment because even if we plant the perfect seed this instant, it will take time to grow and ripen. Ignorance makes us think that we have some control in the moment about whether we have a partner or not. This world view is really very subtle and is the highest correct view (discussed in detail in Step Six).

In summary, ignorance is thinking that doing a misdeed, like lying, will somehow ensure we keep something pleasant, like our partner, or avoid something unpleasant, like our partner's disapproval. And it does appear this way. It seems like our partner stays with us because we have told them we did not cheat. It appears that a lie ensures we keep our partner. When in truth the two actions are not connected. This is why the reality we function in is called deceptive reality. We lie and the next thing that happens is we avoid something unpleasant or we gain something desirable. It appears like cause and effect, but it is not. Logically, and in alignment with the rules of karma, only lying or deception can follow deception. And only fidelity and working to support your own and others' relationships can bring lasting partnership into your life.

The work of the Fifth Step, uncovering the exact nature of our wrongs, can seem like a formidable task. At this point, the wise among my readers have realized that the task is indeed impossible, given basic human limitations of time and ability. However, the Twelve Steps are meant to be practical, not exhausting and as such any efforts made to uncover hidden motives will pay off. Each time we can identify the root of our actions that cause suffering, and subsequently complete Step Six through Step Nine on that problem, we cut that root and are freed from related suffering.

Letting Go of Our Burden

Once we have identified the motivations behind our actions, we proceed to admit these to "all that is", to ourselves and to another human being. The traditional wording of the step has been changed from admitting them to God to admitting them to "all that is" since, in this presentation of the Steps, we purport that God does not exist. However, it is extremely important to admit the exact nature of our wrongs more broadly than to just ourselves and another in order to experience freedom from the past.

In our presentation, "all that is" pretty much covers everything and includes God or any "higher power", god or goddess, spiritual master in spirit form, an enlightened being, the creator, or guardian spirit. It also includes non-personified energies or forces like the universe, all sentient beings, your spiritual source, your creator, universal love. After all, "all that is" is simply everything.

One of the purposes of this step is to draw a line between ourselves and the past behavior that did not serve us. It is important to let go of any guilt, remorse, or regret that is associated with our past. To this end it is important that we hide nothing that we feel bad about. This is the main motivation for confessing. While confessing to another human being is indispensable, we may find that just a confession to one person may leave us with a lingering feeling that somehow we are a "bad" person due to universal law and order. We may think, "Sure, our sponsor accepts us and absolves us, but they have done similar things. Someone else would still condemn us."

In the process of admitting our faults and shortcomings to "all that is", we are most successful in releasing our burden if we envision our admission is received with non-judgment and compassion and we are given acceptance, love and peace in return. To this end, some people find it easier to envision actually making their admission to a "higher power" of their choosing, an enlightened being, or their personal source of refuge.

Step Five, due to the order of the words, instructs us to first admit our wrongs to "all that is" before we admit them even to ourselves. The advantage of first admitting our wrongs to "all that is" is that in connecting with a source that is non-judgmental, we are better able to let go of self-defeating judgments. In Buddhism, there are no rights or wrongs. There are actions and thoughts that do not serve us (negative karma) and those that do (positive karma).

In Step Five we admit not only that we have done things that we do not look upon with satisfaction, but we also admit that beneath each deed has been the basic inclination of grasping to pleasant things/feelings or wanting to avert unpleasantness. The exact nature of all these actions, at the deepest level, is that we have not understood how cause and effect work. Not understanding karma seems to be intrinsically tied up with being human, so in some ways we are really not to blame.

When we first connect with "all that is" we move into a mind-set (or energy-place) that is full of unconditional self-love and non-judgment. This state of being actually allows us to admit more fully to ourselves where we have acted in self-defeating ways.

I have the personal tendency to deny any of my behaviors that I cannot change myself. For instance, when tired, my introversion used to become extreme and I would be short with people and not interact with them like I would when I was not tired. People would call me rude or would think I did not care about them. Certainly I did not do anything morally wrong, but I can see that I planted seeds for people to ignore me or not help me. When I am not connected to my source, I either do not consider the implications of my actions or I defend myself by saying, "I did not do anything wrong." When I am connected to my higher power I can admit what I have done without judgment.

The Four Powers – Destruction Power

Step Four and Step Five combined make up the destruction power described by the Buddha in *The Teaching of the Four Practices*. In this teaching (described completely in Step Ten) the Buddha explains how to kill the mental seeds created from a wrong action. One of the four key forces used is the destruction power.

The destruction power can be described as intelligent regret. It is realizing that what you did is not going to give you a pleasant result and wishing you could take it back. It is not feeling guilt, shame, or worthlessness. All of those things would actually be considered more self-defeating thoughts.

Here is a story that conveys the feeling quality of intelligent regret: Imagine you are in a bar with some buddies and you all order the same type of beverage. Your friend makes a toast and you each begin to drink. Your friend on the left finishes his drink and suddenly grabs at his throat and drops down dead. You turn to the friend on the left and notice his drink is three quarters empty. In the next moment he grabs at his throat and also drops down dead. You look at your drink. It is half finished and you have a moment of "intelligent regret". You wish you had never had that drink, but there is nothing you can do. In the next moment you are dead too.

Intelligent regret is an important part of destruction power. Another important part of this power is confession. Traditionally, this power is completed by admitting to your spiritual buddies your downfall and vowing to practice restraint in the future. This is exactly what we do in Step Five, yet we never hear this step called "confession". In Tibetan Buddhism, the people that are ordained perform a Sojong ceremony twice a month to confess any downfalls and affirm their moral commitments.

Completing Step Five

We complete Step Five when we finish a thorough exploration of the motivations behind our thoughts and actions and then go on to "confess" or admit the exact nature of our actions to "all that is", ourselves, and to another human being. The goal is to get a feeling that we have been completely forgiven and released from our past.

We understand that we can only know a little in any one moment about what motivates our thoughts and actions and that more will be revealed as we work the Steps and practice using a correct world view in our day to day lives. We, however, celebrate the increased self-knowledge gained by working Step Five and anticipate the rewards as we move forward to Step Six and Step Seven.

STEP SIX
Were entirely ready to release all obstacles to peace.

Our work in Step Six is twofold. First, we commit (are entirely ready) to do whatever we need to do to purify the negative karma we have completed. This purification will be the work of steps Seven, Eight and Nine. Second, we deepen our understanding of emptiness and karma and firmly cement in our minds correct world view. This knowledge is the knife that cuts the root of all our character defects and obstacles to peace by providing us with an antidote to the ignorance which poisons our minds. It is impossible for mental afflictions or character defects to occupy the same mind at the same time as correct world view. Now, isn't that a sweet thought?

Being Entirely Ready

In Step Four and Step Five we uncovered thoughts, speech, and actions that resulted in the planting of mental potentials or karmic seeds. We naturally want to have the negative seeds removed now that we understand what will result because of them. Our first task in Step Six is to become entirely ready to release them.

What does it mean to be "entirely ready"?

If we hold that our actions were justified, useful, and right or believe they served us in some way, then it naturally follows that we would not want to give up those aspects of character that support such actions and thoughts. However, the knowledge of how karma works that we have gained by analyzing the ideas presented in this text and reviewing our experience of life will provide us with the motivation necessary to let go of self-defeating aspects of our character. It naturally follows that the preceding steps bring us to a point where we are willing and even eager to rid ourselves of beliefs, thoughts, and behaviors that perpetuate our unhappiness.

Going Deeper

The level of exploration regarding the motivation behind our actions described in Step Five may be sufficient for many, but others may find it helpful to dig even deeper, especially if this is not the first time working the Steps. Many of our more persistent mental afflictions and self-defeating habits were cemented into our subconscious in our youth. As we explore our child-like reactions to certain circumstances we can clear our unconscious drives and find even greater relief.

We start by questioning all of our deep-seated habits. These are often driven by unconscious beliefs. One of the ways that karma seems to manifest is by the beliefs we hold. Wrong beliefs cannot stand up to inspection once they are exposed. They are destroyed by wisdom. It is by bringing our personal motivations into the light that we can actually dispel them – or at least reduce their hold on us.

Our deep questioning leads us to beliefs that are individual and personal. When we ask ourselves, "Why do I do that?" and then listen for the answer we may find that many of the things driving our actions are actually quite absurd when viewed objectively. However, they are very real to the part of us that holds them as true.

Irrational beliefs I have encountered that have driven self defeating behavior include:

- I am not enough.
- I have to earn love.
- I have to take care of my parent's every need.
- I have to please everyone to be happy.
- My drug of choice is my only true friend and takes care of me.
- I have to do "this" to be… happy… loved… taken care of, etc.
- I am unlovable.
- I cannot get angry because if I get angry, I will destroy the world or I will be punished.
- I have to act "this way" to be safe.

Investigating our motivation is important since it is only by knowing ourselves and the way we react that we can become free of unconscious drives. If we continue to react to fear by lying, not only do we still have the fear, but we also have to deal with the consequences of our lying. True freedom is gained by the process of uncovering the beliefs that do not serve us and eradicating them.

It may be of benefit to utilize outside resources if you think deeper work is needed. Use issue-specific books, work in groups with others wishing to get to the root of their problems, and/or get other professional help. Set your intention to clear yourself of self-defeating habits and watch as the necessary resources are delivered to you.

The Four Powers - Restraint Power

Step Six is the foundation of the restraint power in the four forces method for destroying karmic seeds. Restraint power is making a commitment to turn our backs on thoughts and actions that ultimately harm us. Restraining from self-destructive behavior is critical to the final destruction of the karmic seeds that we planted when doing similar self-destructive behavior in the past. In combination with the other three powers, restraint frees us from negative mental potentials (karmic seeds) by destroying them. In a sense, the Four Powers absolve us from our past actions so we can move unfettered into the future.

In Step Six we firmly place in our minds the reasons that our actions hurt us and why we want to avoid them. In Step Seven we complete the restraint power by vowing or pledging to not engage in such self-defeating behavior again.

Once we decide that we are ready to turn our back on our character defects we take on the task of deepening our understanding of how the world works. Knowledge of emptiness will give us the strength to see our commitment through. Presented next is an in-depth explanation of emptiness, also known as correct world view, ultimate reality or ultimate truth.

Correct World View

The Buddha's investigations of the way the world works revealed common misconceptions behind the suffering we all experience. He found our unhappiness is a result of thinking that the world exists in a way it does not really exist. The reality we experience is deceptive reality. Deceptive in the sense that it appears to be one way when it is truly another way. The way things really exist is called ultimate reality. Ultimate reality is hidden from the majority of us.

Since we are unable to experience ultimate reality directly (except in certain meditative states) we are left to describe it by contrast. One of the concepts used to describe ultimate reality is emptiness. When we describe ultimate reality we refer to what it is not – what it is "empty" of.

The idea of something being empty is simple enough, but the concepts we are going to be talking about can get confusing, so first let's analyze exactly what the word "empty" means. Consider for a moment this analogy to explain emptiness:

Imagine you went to a theater to meet some friends. When you got there, the theater was "empty". Maybe you sent the following text message to your friends, "Hey, where are you? I'm at the theater and it is empty."

Now obviously the theater was not "empty". You were there, as were the seats, the lights, the stage, the projector, etc. So when something is "empty" it does not mean that nothing is there. When we talk about something being empty we are always referring to a specific thing being absent. Emptiness is the absence of something. In our theater example the theater was empty of your friends.

In Tibetan Buddhism the thing that is absent is called a **gakja**. The gakja is also referred to as "the object we deny". It is the object we deny exists or we deny is present. It is a thing that does not exist and could never exist. It is the object that ultimate reality is "empty" of.

It is absolutely essential to know what the gakja is, because otherwise how can we determine if it is not there. Our conventional reality is deceptive because gakjas appear real and self-existent. This appearance of existence is what gets us in trouble.

> A **gakja** is a thing that does not exist and could never exist. It is the object that ultimate reality is "empty" of.

The different schools of Ancient Buddhism (See Appendix 1) focused on different gakjas and all the different views are valid and useful. However, this does mean that when someone talks about emptiness they may be referring to a different gakja than you think. It is always prudent to get clarification on what they are referring to. It is important to know what reality is empty of or what object is absent.

The Buddha taught people about emptiness and how really understanding or "realizing" emptiness could lead to personal freedom from suffering and to ultimate peace. He presented a comprehensive world view that explained everything ultimate reality was empty of. This comprehensive view can be hard to grasp, so he also taught key things that reality is empty of. Realization of each of the pieces of ultimate reality leads to greater happiness and peace and also leads to a greater understanding of ultimate reality in its entirety.

The pieces of ultimate reality can be referred to as the different flavors of emptiness or different levels of correct world view. Each flavor has its own gakja. We will consider the following gakjas and their corresponding correct world views:

	Gakja	Correct World View
1)	A permanent thing	Impermanence
2)	Ownership	No control or ownership
3)	Chance	Both us and object from the same cause
4)	Inherent Qualities	Nothing is inherently good or bad
5)	Absolute Problem	50% comes from us, 50% from object
6)	Self-Existence	Creation possible, 100% from us

Gakja #1: Permanence vs. Impermanence

Do you think your car, your computer, or your body will last forever? No, of course not. Yet, this is the crux of the first wrong view. It is a subtle belief that we or the things around us will either last forever or will not change in how they function.

We can gauge how strongly we have this world view by observing our reactions to situations in our life. Consider how you react when things you own break or when people you love decide they want to end their relationship with you, or they die. Possible reactions include peaceful acceptance to blind rage. If we really live in the correct world view of impermanence then when the car gets a flat we do not fly off the handle, we simply do the next right thing.

For example, a couple days ago I looked down to see my Bluetooth earpiece on the ground with the earloop chewed off. Apparently, I dropped it and my little dog found it irresistible. My mind automatically went to how I could have prevented this tragedy. I caught myself in the "wrong view" of believing I could change this moment by thinking about the past. And underneath this tendency to try to "bring back" my earpiece is a belief that it was not time for it to be gone. Part of me thought that if I would have done something different it would still be whole. This is the wrong view of permanence.

Obviously, based on my reaction, I still have a little of the wrong view of permanence left. I also have a lot of correct view. I was able to catch myself at almost the instant my mind went to the past. I did a quick course-correction and told myself that such musings were just a waste of time. This corrective reaction was the result of careful analysis of what really works and decades of practice breaking this and other automatic reactions.

How was I able to break my habit of getting angry when things broke? It was a combination of wanting more peace in my life (Step One), realizing what would bring me more peace (Step Two), and then deciding to practice a new way of life that would bring me more peace (Step Three). My practice involves using my intellect to overcome my automatic reactions.

During my earpiece tragedy, I also noticed that despite a momentary wish to make the earpiece whole again by changing the past, I was not that upset. In my mind, I casually thought I would need to pay another seventy dollars for a new one or I would need to live without it. I evaluated my options almost mindlessly. I had the money, but was not sure if a new earpiece was worth the investment. I concluded that I did not need the Bluetooth at that very moment, so I picked up my damaged device, put it on the table and quietly went back to my work. (Now the earpiece lives with an "organic produce" twist-tie in place of the earloop.)

As we adopt the world view that deeply realizes the impermanence of ourselves and the objects around us we move from angry and/or obsessive reactions when we lose things we value to more mild reactions such as brief sadness and then finally we are not surprised at all when something pleasant ends and do not experience the ending of something as a loss.

In this system, our spiritual development ends in nirvana or complete spiritual awakening. This means that we no longer have any mental afflictions. (A mental affliction is any emotion or thought that disturbs the mind that has it.) We do not stop having anger, regret or sadness when something we like changes or ends by repressing our emotions and becoming numb. The realization of impermanence gives us a greater capacity to enjoy what is around us. We know things will end so we do not cling to them when they do. However, we cannot know ultimate peace with the realization of impermanence only. We need to continue to grow and understand all the flavors of emptiness.

Gakja #2: Ownership/Control

Do you own that shirt you are wearing? Can you say you absolutely control it? When we think of ownership we typically think that the things we own we have control over. We get to decide how they are used, where they are kept and who gets to use them.

"I have a tendency to wear my mind on my sleeve. I have a history of losing my shirt."
– Ed Robertson
Barenaked Ladies

72

Our society supports the idea of ownership, but when we go looking for an object we can truly control we will come back empty-handed. Someday that shirt I own might decide to stay at some event I attend and find itself a new "owner".

The gakjas of ownership and control are a variation on the impermanence theme. Our relationships are constantly changing and only temporary, yet we act as if we can own something permanently. To those of us that have completed the First Step, the idea of having power over something is nonsense. In Step One we learned that our best efforts to control things, including the things we own, were fruitless.

It is tempting to think we have control over things, since most of the time things behave as we expect them and people respect the things we own. Do I own the shirt on my back? Well, yes. I can control when it is used, where it is kept and if it is shared with others. Yet, logical analysis concludes that these types of thoughts are delusional. I could go home tonight, put the shirt in the dirty clothes hamper and find tomorrow that my home burns down and that shirt I controlled is no longer mine.

The scientific method tells us that if we can find one exception to a rule than the rule simply does not hold. When we look for a thing that we can control absolutely we cannot find it. It does not exist. Each and every thing is not under our complete control. We cannot even control our own bodies and minds.

Just like with impermanence, we can gauge how well we have realized this world view by examining our reactions when we are unable to control things we own. When our pen "walks away" or our partner refuses to do what we want, do we get bent out of shape?

The *Alcoholics Anonymous Big Book* (Fourth edition, page 417) says:

> ...acceptance is the answer to all my problems today. When I am disturbed, it is because I find some person, place, thing, or situation – some fact of my life – unacceptable to me, and I can find no serenity until I accept that person, place, thing, or situation as being exactly the way it is supposed to be at this moment.

What is commonly referred to as acceptance in Twelve Step circles is a natural outcropping of correct view. In the Twelve Step literature we are urged to accept things, since they are "exactly the way they are supposed to be". The message behind this is that there is a higher power or God that has made them the way they are and acceptance is the only path to peace, since God is in control, not us.

While acceptance is a very useful path to peace, in our system we do not have a "God" that is in control. Our explanation for how things work is different. Instead of a creator being, we find that things are empty of permanence and empty of being controlled. When we do not accept the way things really are, we lose our peace of mind. We do not believe that our reality is the creation of a god, instead we find that our reality is the result of the marriage of karma and emptiness.

In our model, we do not have short term power, but we do have the ability to "create" our future world by our actions today. We are not all powerful, but we certainly are the creators of our world. In the present moment, though, we have very little influence. Acceptance of all that is happening is the best method of achieving short-term peace and optimizing happiness while we use karmic gardening to plant a brighter tomorrow.

Gakja #3: Chance and Randomness

In this, the third flavor of emptiness, we return to a question we contemplated in Step Two: Is everything random? Is it just luck or chance that we run into people at certain times? Did my computer, made at some factory in a far off land, just happen to be the one that ended up at the store I was shopping at? Is it chance that I am wearing the clothes I am wearing today?

The Chittamatra (mind-only) school of Buddhist thought says no. They say it is impossible for there to be chance encounters because both the observer and the object being observed are created from the same cause (karmic seed). All relationships and encounters are empty of chance.

This is a simple, but unusual idea. The idea is that the physical world we perceive and our senses that are capturing the raw data both arise from the same karmic seed in our mind. Hence, this school of thought is called "mind-only". Indeed, the Buddha taught, "The three realms of existence are merely mind."

This is not to suggest that our world is "all in our heads", meaning not real or just an illusion. Our world is certainly real. This just means that our world is projected from our mind. Surprising as it may be, there is no real scientific evidence that proves that the world exists outside our minds. The traditional analogy used to demonstrate the feasibility of this idea is a dream. In a dream the objects appear solid and real, but upon awakening we realize that the entire scenario was lived out in our minds only.

We have even better modern day examples of how our world might be a projection of our minds. In the movie, *The Matrix,* entire lives are lived based on the neural input of a computer program. People eat, work, play and sleep in a physical reality that is "mind-only". The people are "really" asleep in some nutrient-rich pod being controlled by the computer's neural input. Another example is the movie, *Inception*. In this movie people enter a lucid dream state with others in the same state. The physical world in the dream is definitely real, since bullets can kill.

If the world we experience is a projection of our minds then it naturally follows that we will not be able to find the gakja – anything that happens by chance. The idea that there is order to our world makes intuitive sense. When we realize the truth that all relationships and encounters are empty of chance we gain greater freedom from mental afflictions and a deeper capacity for mystery and joy. Let's explore how that would come about.

This knowledge of emptiness is most useful when we see an angry or rude person in front of us. They are not there by chance, nor are they there because a god is trying to test us (or teach us). They are there because we were angry or rude to someone in the past, which planted a mental potential in our

> A **gakja** is a thing that does not exist and could never exist. It is the object that ultimate reality is "empty" of.

mind, which has now ripened. Since we know what created that angry or rude person in front of us we have a better chance at not being rude back. Not being rude to someone will plant a mental potential for us to see people being patient with us in the future.

Nice. Knowledge of the emptiness of chance will result in less unpleasant feelings and more pleasant ones. It also fuels us to continue to act in ways that will create a more pleasant future. Further, when good things happen to us, we can smile with appreciation knowing exactly where the pleasurable experience is coming from.

The only mystery left is the timing on when our seeds ripen. However, we can rest assured that our lives will become nicer and nicer as we continue with thoughtful karmic gardening.

Gakja#4: Inherent Qualities

The idea that something can be judged as absolutely good or absolutely bad results in a great deal of arguing and suffering. Logical analysis will quickly reveal that nothing is inherently bad or good. The qualities of good and bad are projected onto objects based on our own perspectives. The "bad" person that is rude to me at the grocery store is the "good" son that is shopping for his mother. In truth he is neither "good" or "bad" inherently.

Even things that appear initially all bad, such as killing, can be viewed from different perspectives. A story is told of one of the Buddha's earlier incarnations (a Jataka Tale) where he was a ship's captain. In the story he finds out a passenger on the boat is going to do something that will result in everyone on board dying. It is said that in order to save the person from the negative results of such an act, the future buddha murdered the person himself. (Interesting, his mind was not on protecting the lives of the other passengers, but on the fate of the plotting murderer.)

The action of the future buddha resulted in a mixture of mental potentials. He planted the potential to be killed in the future and also the potential to be saved from being killed. Was what he did "good" or "bad"? Well, the whole point is to understand that there is nothing that is inherently good or bad. Any analysis with the intention of determining ultimate "goodness" is a waste of time. Everything we do will give us a mixture of pleasant and unpleasant results.

The way we judge the depth of our understanding regarding this flavor of emptiness is by how strongly we hold to our position of good or bad. If we get angry at people for doing things the wrong way we are focused on a gakja, since there is no inherently right way to do things. If we are invested in proving our point or having everyone agree with our ideas, then we are clinging to the wrong view of things being inherently right.

One last interesting point about this world view is how it impacts our work in Step Six. In Step Six we are becoming ready to release our defects of character, yet this world view suggests that there is no such thing as an inherently bad defect of character. Indeed, we may notice that many of our character traits can be used in ways that either serve us well or contribute to our detriment.

Gakja #5: Absolute Problem

Our next gakja is a problem that is one hundred percent problem. We are denying that there is anything that is all problem. While you are busy trying to find one, let me give you the background on the Buddhist school of thought that will be used to explain why you will not be able to find a problem that is an absolute, complete problem.

The position we will be taking is that of the Svatantrika (independent) school of Buddhist thought. (See Appendix 1 for a breakdown of Buddhist schools of thought.) This view is an extension of the idea that there are no inherent qualities of an object. For Gakja #5, we are saying that the object is not inherently the same object for everyone. In other words, a problem is not inherently a problem.

According to the Svatantrikas, when we experience a problem (or any object) it is because the problem (or object) appears to us and we perceive it as a problem (or specific object). That

> **Reframing** is considering an event or object and determining alternate views or explanations of it.

is the bottom line. A problem comes fifty percent from the object and fifty percent from our perspective of the object.

The best explanation of this level of emptiness is that used extensively by Geshe Michael Roach. He uses the example of a pen. Let's consider a pen from the point of view of the Svatantrikas.

When you are viewing a pen, what is really happening is that a cylindrical object "appears" to you. At the same time you "see" the cylinder as a pen. Fifty percent of the "pen" comes from the cylinder that appears to you and fifty percent of the "pen" is you seeing the object as a pen.

To really understand this view, consider the same pen when a dog walks in the room. The cylinder appears to the dog, but the dog does not see a pen. Based on his karmic propensity, he sees a chew toy. So you see a pen to write with and a dog sees a toy to chew on. The cylindrical object has no inherent qualities. The same raw data presents to both us and the dog, but what each of us brings in the form of karma results in two different things being perceived.

Indeed, Geshe Michael Roach tells us that the only difference between us and the dog is the karmic seeds that are ripening and resulting in the projection we see. The dog has seeds to see the cylinder as a chew toy and the seeds to see his limbs as legs and paws. We have the karma to see the cylinder as a pen and our limbs as arms, legs, hands and feet.

In the fourth world view, a pen was neither good nor bad. Here we learn that a pen is not inherently a pen, but could be a chew toy depending on the viewer. How can this world view help us? This world view allows for the process of reframing. **Reframing** is looking at an event or object and determining alternate views or explanations of it.

In my book, *The Answers Are Within,* I tell the story of reframing being robbed on Christmas Eve. I felt horribly violated when someone took fifteen dollars from my car, although I would have willingly given the same amount to someone in need. Since there was nothing I could do to change the situation, imagining the robber to be a honorable person in great need was how I reframed the event to gain more personal peace.

People in program use reframing a lot. It is a great technique to lessen the impact of the unpleasant events in our lives that we cannot control. We become thankful for inconveniences by imagining worse things that could have happened. For

> "...for there is nothing either good or bad, but thinking makes it so."
> -Shakespeare

instance, we imagine the flat tire or red light are ways we were protected from a head-on collision that might have happened in the next block. Or we are grateful for negative encounters with people because they are helping us develop patience or compassion.

✗ As we have moved up the levels of emptinesses we have learned:

1. Things do not last forever.

2. We have no control over events or things.

3. Our experiences are no accident.

4. Things are only good or bad if we label them so.

5. Things are not even things until we label them.

All these useful views of the world can increase our happiness and peace. Yet, even this fifth view leaves us short. Unpleasant things are still happening to us. A flat tire is still no fun even if it helped us avoid a lethal collision.

Gakja #6: Self-Existence

The sixth world view is the complete picture. It is the view that will allow us to destroy all our mental afflictions and realize everlasting peace. The ultimate view is that everything comes from us and our projections. There is no raw data out there that is appearing to us and suggesting to us that it is a pen or some other object. This higher view is an extension of the mind-only perspective, except now we consider the mind, and even karma, as projections as well. No object or self exists independently.

The ultimate reality that nothing exists independently is a little hard to conceptualize. We tend to think linearly and we need a starting point to do so. Dependent origination suggests a cyclical process. How do you talk about karmic seeds or even the notion of emptiness when they are just projections? And who is projecting if no-self exists?

Dependent Origination means that nothing exists independently. All things exist based on something else. Three views of dependent origination are:

Functionalists – things are dependent on their causes

Independents – things are dependent on their parts

Consequence - things are dependent on you calling them and thinking of them as you do.

Functionalists, Independents and Consequence are three schools of Buddhist thought. More information in Appendix 1.

Ultimately we need to understand and realize this world view. This will happen naturally as we progress along our spiritual path. First, we will gain a good intellectual understanding of correct world view and automatically cultivate a spiritual practice that is in alignment with it. Deep realization can occur gradually or can result from a dramatic direct experience of ultimate reality (this highest definition of emptiness) during specific meditative states.

In this world view nothing lasts conventionally longer than an instant and everything is a result of causes and conditions. "We" are what is behind the causes and conditions that create our world. This is the good news. If we are one hundred percent responsible for our world, then our salvation is possible. If unpleasant things are even one percent coming from somewhere else we do not have a chance of breaking completely free. Only if we are one hundred percent responsible for everything in our world will we be able to end our suffering and the suffering of those around us.

In practice, this world view immediately provides us with increased happiness and peace, because finally we have the control over our destiny which we have been hoping for. We still have no control in the moment, because the things happening right now are the result of our previous thoughts and actions. However, we are like an imprisoned person that realizes that there is a way to escape. It may take some time, but the means are available and a bright future awaits us.

In the fifth world view, when irritating people enter our lives we use our intellect to reframe the situations so we can experience greater peace. For instance, when a driver cuts us off in traffic we imagine they are the sweetest of people and they are rushing to get to their dying mother. This view softens our heart and lessens or even removes our irritation.

In the sixth world view we realize that as we practice patience (and we still use reframing to help) we will completely eliminate opportunities to be patient in the future. We know that when someone yells at us and we do not yell back we are eliminating angry people from our lives. Upon perfecting patience, there will no longer be people in our lives to be patient with. They will have ceased to exist for us because we have eliminated their cause.

I have a personal example to illustrate how this works. I once took a job working at a recovery center. Right after I was hired the facility changed owners and management. The health and wellness coordinator position I held did not match the new organization's treatment philosophy and I found myself in a position without any support and not integrated with the rest of the staff. I felt like an outsider and just before they fired me they actually moved me from my central office to the second floor of a distant building.

I watched as the job I took and the environment I was hired into completely changed. I knew I was one hundred percent responsible for what I was experiencing and at the same time powerless to change things in "real" time. What I did, using a list of both staff and clients, was spend a good deal of my day applying an Ancient Hawaiian technique for clearing karma called Ho'oponopono.

Ho'oponopono was made popular by a psychiatric doctor who used this prayer method to shut down a mental hospital he worked at in Hawaii. The hospital, originally unsafe, full of criminally insane patients and poorly coping staff, was closed after a period of a few years. As he prayed, the patients got better and the facility became safe. Using what we are calling the sixth world view he eliminated from his life a hospital full of crazy people.

The Ho'oponopono method includes all the components of the Buddhist method of the four practices, but focuses on cleaning up general offenses involving specific people. Since my situation was generally unpleasant, I mimicked the practice of the psychiatric doctor. As I cleared, the negative situation was indeed removed from my life. I was fired.

This was not necessarily the most pleasant of outcomes, except it resulted in me ending up in a dream environment. At my next job I had two incredibly supportive bosses, I worked with a team of exceptionally dedicated and caring co-workers, and I felt completely supported and included – just the opposite of the position I left. There was not one unpleasant staff person to deal with. This is how the sixth world view works in practice.

The Marriage of Karma and Emptiness

Emptiness tells us that all objects and situations, including ourselves, are empty of any independent self-existence. This sounds like nothing exists – which is not true at all. The things in our world are real and do exist. The definition of existence is that something appears to us and that we perceive it with an unimpaired mind. (Unimpaired meaning not on drugs or dreaming or under the influence of an optical illusion.)

The catch is that while things do exist, they are existing deceptively. They appear to be self-existent, when in truth they are projections of our personal karma. This is where we get into the marriage of karma and emptiness. You cannot have one without the other.

It is because the world around us is empty that karma is able to work. Emptiness is like the blank screen the movie is played on. Karma is what projects the movie. The movie is real in this theater of life and it is where we get the opportunity to create.

Avoiding the Two Extremes

The Middle Way sages say:

Nothing exist naturally, but not that nothing exists at all.

Everything exist merely by convention , but everything exists without existing naturally.

In teachings about emptiness the words naturally, truly, really and absolutely are all terms that refer to something that is self-existent. They are all referring to the gakja. This verse is telling us that things do not exist out there all by themselves in ultimate reality, but they do exist and function in our deceptive reality.

This verse is a reminder for us to avoid the two extremes. The first extreme is that of nihilism. It is the belief that nothing really exists. The nihilist thinks, "Everything is empty, which means nothing exists. It follows that I can do whatever I please without any consequence." The second extreme is that of eternalism. It is the belief that everything exists independently. The eternalist thinks, "Everything exists and is solid and fixed. I can only affect such things by external effort."

Neither view is correct or useful. Things do exist conventionally and we cannot affect them by external effort, unless those efforts are supported by the corresponding mental potentials. The view of emptiness and dependent origination we have been describing is referred to as the Middle Way. It is a balanced view that avoids the downfalls inherent in the two extremes of nihilism and eternalism.

Completing Step Six

Initially, what we would really like to accomplish with Step Six is a solid understanding of the different flavors of emptiness. However, ultimately we need to have a deep realization of correct world view. Understanding means we intellectually accept and appreciate the different ideas. Realization is an even deeper understanding arising from direct experience. Upon having a realization of correct world view, all of our actions will naturally flow from and are based on correct world view. Realization of the different world views is referred to as the achievement of wisdom. As we gain wisdom all of our character traits are directed towards benefitting ourselves and others.

We complete Step Six when we have reviewed what stands in our way of achieving lasting peace, our character defects and patterns of motivation, and understand that both of these are founded and maintained on wrong views. Although, we may not have a complete understanding of emptiness, we identified with one of the six "flavors", and can see how adopting the corresponding correct view would reduce our problems. As for our past deeds, we understand how they will create our future and are eager to destroy the seeds we created by refraining from the same actions in the future. We move on to Step Seven willing to turn our backs on self-defeating behaviors.

STEP SEVEN
Humbly dedicated ourselves to the path.

Traditionally, this is a fairly passive step where all we do is ask to have our shortcomings removed and then God takes it from there. The originators of the Twelve Steps understood that when it comes down to it, we are powerless over our shortcomings and that transforming them requires nothing short of divine intervention. In the original wording of the step, "humbly asked Him to remove our shortcomings", we ask for help with our shortcomings, because we know we cannot control ourselves.

If you are not convinced that you do not have control over yourself, stop reading for a moment, close your eyes and bring your focus to your breath. Then, keep your awareness *solely* on your breath for five minutes. If you have had some training you may be able to do this. I cannot do it, even with over a decade of training.

This exercise demonstrates that we have very little control over ourselves, but each of us probably has additional evidence. In a moment of anger or irritation, we forget to be kind and say things we later wish we would not have. And many of us know intimately the experience of not wanting to pick up our drug of choice, yet being compelled to do so. The powerlessness we explored in the First Step extends to even ourselves. We simply cannot eliminate our shortcomings by wishing them gone.

If we are unable to control ourselves and a higher power is not available to help us, then how do we get rid of these pesky shortcomings? Well, the work is really all ours. We understand now that what we are experiencing in the present moment as shortcomings is the result of our past deeds, thoughts and actions. We are powerless over our impulses and reactions at the moment they happen. However, we do have the power to plant new mental potentials that will ultimately result in the elimination of our shortcomings. This is the path we dedicate ourselves to in Step Seven.

This karmic gardening takes time. Hence the wording of Step Seven is to *humbly dedicate* ourselves to the path. We understand now where our character defects are coming from and how only perseverance will allow us to enjoy a transformation of character. Like the original intention of this step, we do our part with a humble dedication, continue our path of self transformation by working the remaining steps and let "divine" timing determine when and how we will reap the fruit of our labor. We cannot control, in the short run, which karmic seeds running around in our psyche will be triggered.

We dedicate ourselves to spiritual growth and are not overly concerned about the timing of the outcome. Step Seven, like Step Three, has the flavor of surrender. Knowing what is right, and doing what is right, are two different things. We may not have the power to always do the right thing – that power is given to us by our past actions and thoughts, but as we continue to practice, each day trying to align ourselves as best we can to correct world view, we will find that we are more and more able to do the right thing.

This transformation of our character appears to many of us as a welcome miracle. In actuality, it is merely the result of our practice. Our intention and repeated attempts to do the right thing creates powerful mental potentials that then force us to see a more pleasant world around us. Just like our karmic seeds forced us to see ourselves falling short of our ideals before, we are now forced to see ourselves responding intelligently in difficult situations.

Indeed, the difficult situations themselves are also transformed. We just do not see things the same way. We are no longer reacting; we are acting. Our mental afflictions are diminished and we experience more of the beauty and joy of life. The flowers, birds and love were there all along, but now we are able to enjoy them.

The Four Powers – Restraint Power

In Step Six we deepened our understanding of how our past actions and deeds create our present. With this knowledge in hand, we became entirely ready to firmly turn our backs on a manner of living that is self-defeating.

In Step Seven we complete the power of restraint by dedicating ourselves to the elimination of wrong view and wrong action. Further, we begin to cultivate the power of the antidote by undertaking a manner of living based on correct view and correct action. We understand that this new way of living will lead to greater productivity in the world and greater peace and happiness. This knowledge motivates us.

Completing Step Seven

We complete Step Seven by dedicating ourselves to the process of self transformation. This dedication may take the form of a simple proclamation such as:

> I dedicate myself to my spiritual path. I am committed to the complete elimination of all aspects of character that stand in the way of my usefulness to self and others. I dedicate myself to the cultivation and development of character traits that will be for the highest benefit of myself and everyone I come in contact with.

We may also vow or pledge to refrain from the Ten Misdeeds while seeking to carry out the Ten Virtues. There are also formal vows or precepts that Buddhists can take as part of their religious tradition. Since we know that there is no being that can remove our shortcomings, there is further action we must engage in. Affirming our commitment, we move quickly to complete the remaining steps.

STEP EIGHT
Made a list of all persons we had harmed, and became willing to make amends to them all.

In Step Eight we make our list of people we have harmed in preparation for making amends. The inspiration for our list primarily comes from the inventory completed in Step Four. However, we may decide to include people that we resent due to things *they* have said or done, even if *we* have behaved ethically towards them.

Many resentments may have dropped away as we have worked our way through the Steps and gained a deeper knowledge of emptiness and how our world and the people in it are created. This is only natural. The remaining people or institutions we resent are added to our list not because we need to apologize to them, but because we will want to amend (improve) our relationship with them. This is not for their benefit, although though they may benefit. It is for our own increased happiness and peace of mind. Resentment and bitterness are states of mind that primarily disturb us.

Include All Sentient Beings
In Tibetan, the word for "people" includes all beings, so in Step Eight we also consider the harm we have caused to animals and insects. A sentient being is considered any being that can feel and respond. This certainly includes animals and insects.

But what about bacteria, viruses and plants? Single-celled bacteria can be seen to respond to their environment by moving away from toxins and toward nutrients. This would suggest sentience in the most basic form. Viruses, in contrast, do not exhibit this same "consciousness".

Plants also have the ability to feel and respond, yet they are typically considered non-living in Buddhist circles. Indeed, while in English we talk about a plant *dying*, in Tibetan they say a plant *dries up*. Since plants are not living, yet they obviously grow, their "expansion" is considered to follow the same growth pattern as that of mineral crystals.

If plants and rocks are not living, why do many people of earth-based spiritual traditions consider them so? Often, in such traditions it is the plant spirits or the spirit of the rocks that are interacted with and not the plant or mineral itself. Tibetans do honor and respect nature spirits. Spirits are certainly sentient beings.

From a Tibetan Buddhist perspective our list of "people" would include animals and insects, but not plants. However, it is important to realize that harm to plants, rocks and our environment ultimately harms other sentient beings. Grasping the full impact of our actions is not intended to burden us with guilt, but instead to inspire us to action. By our actions we can create greater harmony in the world. This calls us to act with respect towards all things.

Due to our study of emptiness, we understand that an action to harm any living being will result in future harm to ourselves unless we undertake purification. We also understand that when we are focused on protecting life, including the environment that supports life, this benefits us. The ultimate result of protecting life is the end of our own suffering and freedom from death. Consideration for all things, living and non-living, is wisdom.

Bodhichitta

|སེམས་བསྐྱེད་པ་ནི་གཞན་དོན་ཕྱིར། །ཡང་དག་རྫོགས་པའི་བྱང་ཆུབ་འདོད།

The short definition of bodhichitta written in Tibetan

Bodhichitta is the state of single-pointed desire to reach Buddhahood in order to help every living being do the same. At first glance, developing bodhichitta may seem unrelated to the work of the Eighth Step. After all, we are only making a list of the people we have harmed and becoming willing to make amends to them. However, according to the sixth world view, everyone we know or have heard about belongs on the list since they and their condition are projected by us. Completely cleaning up our misdeeds, which is the intention of Steps Eight and Nine, would result in ultimate amends – the end of everyone's suffering.

Wow! Everyone goes on our list? Including the people harmed by last month's natural disaster in a distant land? Yes, everyone goes on our list. This is a bit of a stretch for most of us – and a true test of our understanding of emptiness. Remember, in the sixth flavor of emptiness, we are one hundred percent responsible for everything we encounter. Everything is coming from us. This means that if we see someone suffering, a little or a lot, we are ultimately responsible.

Bodhichitta, the highest wish for enlightenment, is where we wish to not only end our own suffering but the suffering of all beings. When one has fully developed loving-kindness and great compassion and holds an almost obsessive desire to end other peoples' suffering, one naturally realizes the best way to do so is to reach complete enlightenment, or Buddhahood. Complete enlightenment is reached when we end our own suffering with the wish that others also be free.

When one has a sincere and complete realization of bodhichitta, one becomes a bodhisattva. A bodhisattva is a spiritual warrior. A bodhisattva carries in their heart and mind the highest wish for enlightenment. All of a bodhisattva's actions arise from this intention and support this goal, hence even ordinary activities like brushing one's teeth are seen as great virtues if you are a bodhisattva. Indeed, becoming a bodhisattva is perhaps the greatest way to make amends to the multitudes of people that are suffering around us. So how do we do it?

> **Bodhichitta** is the wish to achieve total enlightenment for the sake of others.

Prerequisite for Developing Bodhichitta

Pabongka Rinpoche[4], in his commentary on Je Tsongkapa's *Three Principal Paths*, describes a seven step cause and effect method for developing bodhichitta. The prerequisite for using this method is developing a state of neutrality toward all beings. Such neutrality can be developed in a number of ways, but Pabongka Rinpoche describes a method based on a belief in reincarnation.

Reincarnation is not a common childhood teaching in the West and perhaps you do not believe it. As stated earlier, never believe anything blindly that insults your intellect. If you are unsure about a claim, take the time to consider its validity using logic, personal experience or the endorsement of a trusted authority. Certain cultures are taught as children

---

[4] Pabongka Rinpoche (1878-1941) was a highly influential teacher in Tibet. He was the root lama of the two tutors of the present Dalai Lama and many other Gelugpa lamas. His most renowned work is "Liberation in our Hands" which he taught to an audience of over 700 people over the period of twenty-four days.

about past and future lives, but just because your mother says it is so does not necessarily make it true.

Reincarnation can be logically explained as described in Master Dharmakirti's[5] *Commentary on Valid Perception*, which is based on an earlier work by Buddhist logic pioneer, Master Dignaga[6]. However, in order to accept the outcome of their argument in support of reincarnation, one must first be convinced that mind can only come from mind. I refer readers to the Asian Classics Institute's *Course IV: The Proof of Future Lives* for a full presentation of the arguments.

For our purposes we will assume that mind can only come from mind. Now, if mind can only come from mind, then one can trace backwards each moment of mind starting from the present. For instance, there was a moment

> Mind is defined as a thing that is invisible and aware.

of mind that preceded the present moment of mind and a moment of mind that proceeded that. When we get to our birth in this current physical form we realize that the mind had to have come from a similar mind that immediately preceded that "newborn" moment of mind.

Tibetan Buddhists use this process to go back lifetime after lifetime and conclude that the mind never had a beginning since it always had to come from a moment of mind that preceded it. Trained meditators can actually do this process of following the mindstream backwards. The conclusion is we have been reincarnating since beginningless time.

Developing Neutrality Towards All Others

Since we have had countless lives, it is possible that we have been every type of sentient being and each gender innumerable times. Your best friend in this life may have been your best friend, or enemy, or father, or daughter, or uncle, or boss, or some other relation many, many times in the past. We develop a neutral feeling towards all beings because we see that our current opinion about each person we know is transitory and based on a role they are playing that will change sooner or later.

Indeed, many of us have had the experience in just this one life of a friend becoming an enemy or someone we disliked becoming a friend. We do not need to consider the reincarnation argument to realize that when

---

[5] Master Dharmakirti (c. 630AD), an Indian Buddhist, was one of the leaders in Buddhist logic thought but also held views consistent with mind only and Madhyamika schools.

[6] Master Dignaga (c. 450AD) authored the foundational works for Buddhist logic. He was an Indian Buddhist and the student of Master Vasubandhu (the author of Abhidharmakosa –The Treasure House of Knowledge).

push comes to shove, some unlikely sentient being may come to our rescue and some friend may disappoint us. Since roles are transitory, it may help to imagine your enemy is just pretending to be so – they are like an actor in a play. In the next scene they may play the role of your best friend. Such a perspective helps us achieve a neutral view of others.

This contemplation, whether we are using the reincarnation model or reflecting on relationships in our current life, is designed to eliminate our bias and restore a sense of neutrality or non-judgment towards other beings. If these methods do not work for you, perhaps you can think of a personal way to develop the needed attitude of neutrality.

In a practical sense, the process of reframing is being used here. We are not using ultimate world view but instead find ourselves in the fifth world view described in Step Six. We are thinking about the beings around us and considering an alternate view of them instead of "friend" or "enemy". It is certainly a reframing process that allows us to imagine that unlikable person we are about to get mad at is a dear friend that saved our life in the past or someone who may save our life in the future.

We can also use the same reframing process without the reincarnation model if we desire. We simply imagine that the person we are about to get mad at is going through a difficult period and is doing the best they can. Or we can think of some other great story, customized to soften our heart, that would remove us from a judgmental state of mind and bring us back to a neutral state of mind.

I personally like to connect to the humanness of the person I am judging. I examine my past, looking for instances when I behaved the same way or I behaved in a way not in alignment with correct world view and did something that really did not serve me. For instance, my favorite line when someone cuts me off in traffic is, "I've done that before" or "They are driving just like me!"

Seven Step Method for Generating Bodhichitta

Once we have developed a feeling of neutrality toward each living being, the first step of the method described by Pabongka Rinpoche follows automatically. After we recognize that each being has been our father, daughter, uncle, friend, enemy, or neighbor countless times:

 1. We recognize that every being has been our mother once or many times. (Imagine each being as the ideal mother – for in countless lifetimes every being was an exceptional mother at least once.) Then we consider what each being, as our ideal mother, did for us. As our mother, each being devoted hours to our care and endured the discomfort of pregnancy, childbirth, sleepless nights, cleaning

up our feces, urine and more. They loved us, worried about us, and cared for us to the best of their ability – often making personal sacrifices. Once we realize that each being has been our mother and what they did for us in that role it follows naturally that...

 We feel gratitude for their kindness. And as we reflect on our gratitude for their kindness,

 We want to repay their kindness. We then reflect on ways to repay their kindness.

 As a natural result of the first three steps, we develop complete loving-kindness for all beings. We begin to feel deep love for each being. We love each being as if they are our own children. This love is a feeling or obsession to make them happy.

 But then we realize they are suffering. We know that they cannot receive things to make them happy until their pain is removed. The people of the world are like a mother at her child's funeral – completely overcome with pain. They cannot enjoy things that usually make them happy while they are full of grief and pain. This leads to feelings of great compassion. Great compassion is the wish to remove everyone's suffering. From this contemplation it naturally follows that...

 We decide that we will work hard to remove everyone's pain and sorrow. We take it upon ourselves to do it – even if no one else will help. It is too important to do and we cannot wait around for others to get motivated to help.

 We realize that we can really only accomplish the previous step if we completely end our own suffering. We need to be able to do it first ourselves in order to help other people do it. We also know that only gaining the omniscience of a buddha will allow us to truly know how to help people. Completing this step results in the realization of bodhichitta.

Bodhichitta is considered a higher spiritual attainment then lesser forms of enlightenment. This is because with bodhichitta we make a commitment to help the multitude of sentient beings all achieve enlightenment.

Summary of Seven Step Method for Generating Bodhichitta

1. Recognize all beings as one's mother
2. Feel gratitude for their kindness
3. Wish to repay that kindness
4. Loving-kindness towards all beings (Desire that they are happy)
5. Great Compassion (The desire that all beings are free of suffering)
6. Resolve to personally help everyone, even if no one else helps
7. Bodhichitta – The desire to become a buddha to benefit all beings

---

The Four Powers – The Power of Antidote

The power of the antidote is the final force used to completely destroy the potentials created by negative thoughts and actions. Step Three gave us our foundation power – taking refuge in an understanding of karma and emptiness. Step Four and Step Five supplied us the power of destruction – cultivating a healthy regret for doing things that would come back to harm us personally. Step Six and Step Seven provided the power of restraint – pledging to turn our back on wrong action. Now we apply the final force, the power of the antidote, by undertaking Step Eight and Step Nine.

The antidote power is the strongest force of the Four Powers. It is critical to the process of destroying our negative potentials. Antidote power is achieved by undertaking some activity designed to make up for the wrong action or thought.

There are two parts to any make up activity. One part involves direct amends and the other is an activity that works to purify the mind. Making amends is integral to the Twelve Steps as we know them. It is also a component of ethical living. In the Twelve Steps, we make direct amends for our actions in Step Nine. We call this action "keeping our side of the street clean".

The other part of the antidote power is emphasized in the commentaries on the Buddha's *Teaching of the Four Practices*. A make up activity is the antidote for the poisonous seed we have created in our mind. There are a number of traditional make up activities that serve as an antidote. These include:

- Studying emptiness

- Reciting secret words of power (mantras)

- Making images of enlightened beings

- Making offerings

- Other practices such as prayer and recitation

These activities are meant to strengthen our resolve to live in a manner that will be for our own highest benefit. They are designed to help us connect to our spiritual source and inspiration. Of all of the make up activities, studying emptiness is considered the highest, since it is the wisdom that comes from knowing emptiness that actually gives us the power to change. Knowledge of emptiness is the antidote that cures the poison of our past deeds.

One Possible Antidote – The Heart Sutra

The Heart Sutra is a teaching on emptiness. It actually encompasses three of the traditional make-up activities: 1) The sutra is studied to help with the understanding of emptiness, 2) it is recited as a blessing and to remove obstacles, and 3) the sutra itself contains the Prajna Paramita Mantra. This mantra can be recited alone or as part of the recitation of the sutra.

The sutra is actually a conversation between two of the Buddha's high-level students while in his presence. In the end, the Buddha acknowledges the validity of the teaching by saying "true" three times.

> **Prajna Paramita** – is Sanskrit for the perfection of wisdom. It is the direct experience of emptiness.

The conversation centers on the realization and importance of understanding emptiness. In the sutra, Avalokiteshvara Bodhisattva (the first student) comes out of deep meditation where he was experiencing emptiness directly (a.k.a. the prajna paramita) and begins explaining his experience to Shariputra (the second student).

Avalokiteshvara (a.k.a. Loving Eyes) realizes that all five skandhas are empty. Skandha is a Sanskrit term that is used to describe all the parts that make up a human being. It is translated to English as either aggregate or heap. We are made up of five heaps: 1) form, 2) feelings, 3) perceptions, 4) formations, and 5) consciousness. These five heaps, or five aggregates, can be further described as follows:

1. Form – refers to all the parts of our physical body.

2. Feelings – refers to the feelings of pleasant, unpleasant or neutral.

3. Perceptions – is actually better translated as discrimination. It refers to the ability to distinguish between things, like this is red and that is blue.

4. Formations – is a catch all "heap" of things that are not covered in the other four heaps. It refers to all the other mental functions besides feelings and perceptions. In addition it includes things that

are neither mental nor physical such as ideas or concepts, like the concept of "Dorena" or "John".

5.   Consciousness – includes our six forms of consciousness. These are the five sense consciousness (seeing, hearing, smelling, tasting, feeling) and the main mind consciousness. Sometimes this heap is called awareness.

In the first words Avalokiteshvara speaks, he stresses four relationships:

- Form does not differ from emptiness.

- Emptiness does not differ from form.

- That which is form is emptiness.

- That which is emptiness, form.

He is speaking quite poetically and almost redundantly, but there are some subtle differences in the four relationships. Basically, the first relationship is saying that "your body is empty". This means your body is dependent on your karmic projections and does not exist independently. The second relationship can be rephrased as the reciprocal, "emptiness is your body". This is not possible. Your body is a changing, positive thing and emptiness is an unchanging, negative thing that is part of ultimate reality. (Negative, meaning it is the *absence* of something.) What he is emphasizing is that the body you experience is due to karmic projections. In other words, the emptiness of your body allows your body to exist. The third relationship refers to the fact that we must have a body to have the emptiness of the body. If the body exists, then so does its emptiness. While emptiness is unchanging it is also not permanent. The body is created simultaneously with its emptiness and when the body ceases to exist its emptiness also ceases to exist. Each object has its own emptiness that is identical to all the other emptinesses. The fourth relationship stresses that the body would not exist without emptiness. Form must be empty in order for the karmic projections to "show".

These four relationships hold true for the other four heaps that make up a person. All five skandhas are empty. Avalokiteshvara goes on to emphasize that all dharmas are marked with emptiness. Dharma can refer to the teachings of the Buddha, but it can also mean "thing". In this context, he is saying "all *things* are marked with emptiness". What he means by "they do not appear nor disappear, are neither tainted nor pure, do not increase nor decrease" is that these things do not occur independently. Sure things appear and disappear, just not independently.

Their emptiness ensures that their characteristics are dependent on our karmic projections.

Just in case we did not get that everything exists dependent on our projections, Avalokiteshvara goes on a tirade: There is no (*self-existent*) form, no feelings, no perceptions, no formations, no consciousness, no eyes, no ears, no nose, no tongue...no path, no cognition and no attainment. Nothing exists independently because of emptiness. Indeed, the reference to "no suffering, no origination, no stopping, and no path" is saying that even the Four Noble Truths are dependent.

The next two verses stress that this wisdom of emptiness (the prajna paramita) is all one needs to become a buddha and every self-respecting bodhisattva depends on it. In the end he utters the mantra:

Gate, Gate, Paragate, Parasamgate! Bodhi! Svaha!!
Go,   Go,   Go far,   Go far beyond! Buddhahood!   Yes!!

This mantra also can be interpreted as referring to the five realizations that one must have to become enlightened. The first "Go" means reach the path of accumulation where, in part, you have the realization of renunciation and bodhichitta. The second "Go" means reach the path of preparation where you achieve a good intellectual understanding of emptiness. "Go far" means reach the path of seeing (the direct perception of no-self, emptiness, or ultimate reality). "Go far beyond" refers to the path of habituation where you become accustomed to the wisdom gained at the path of seeing. The final path is that of "no more learning" or Buddhahood.

The Five Paths (Realizations)

1. Path of Accumulation – true renunciation and bodhichitta
2. Path of Preparation – deep intellectual understanding of emptiness
3. Path of Seeing – direct experience of ultimate reality or emptiness
4. Path of Habituation – using correct view to eliminate mental afflictions
5. Path of No More Learning – buddhahood

Here is a short version of the Heart Sutra that is good for recitation. In the longer version, material regarding the circumstances surrounding this teaching and the endorsement by the Buddha is included.

The Exalted One, the Lady of Conquest, the Sutra on the Heart of the Perfection of Wisdom

Avalokiteshvara Bodhisattva when practicing deeply the prajna paramita, perceives that all five skandhas are empty and is saved from all suffering and distress.

"O Shariputra, form does not differ from emptiness, emptiness does not differ from form. That which is form is emptiness, that which is emptiness form.

The same is true of feelings, perceptions, formations, consciousness.

O Shariputra, all dharmas are marked with emptiness; they do not appear nor disappear, are not tainted nor pure, do not increase nor decrease.

Therefore in emptiness,
no form, no feelings, no perceptions, no formations, no consciousness;
no eyes, no ears, no nose, no tongue, no body, no mind;
no color, no sound, no smell, no taste, no touch, no object of mind;
no realm of eyes until no realm of mind-consciousness;
no ignorance and also no extinction of it until no old-age-and-death and also no extinction of it; no suffering, no origination, no stopping, no path;
no cognition, also no attainment.

With nothing to attain, a bodhisattva depends on prajna paramita and the mind is no hindrance. Without any hindrance no fears exist. Far apart from every perverted view one dwells in nirvana.

In the three worlds all buddhas depend on prajna paramita and attain unsurpassed complete perfect enlightenment.

Therefore, know the prajna paramita is the great transcendent mantra, is the great bright mantra, is the utmost mantra, is the supreme mantra, which is able to relieve all suffering and is true, not false.

So proclaim the prajna paramita mantra, proclaim the mantra that says:

Gate, Gate, Paragate, Parasamgate! Bodhi! Svaha!"

Completing Step Eight

We complete Step Eight when we have in hand a list of the people and beings we have harmed and the willingness in our heart to make things right. There may remain some people on the list that we hold bitterness towards or reservations about admitting we were wrong. Our continued study of emptiness, one of the most powerful make up activities, will soon dispel any lingering reservations. Correct world view will replace our misconceptions and we will realize that our future freedom depends on positive actions today. Amending relationships and working to undo the harm we have done to others will unfetter us from negative karmic potentials. We proceed to Step Nine ready to make direct amends to many of the people on the list and with greater optimism of our future.

STEP NINE
Made direct amends to such people wherever possible except when to do so would injure them or others.

As we go out to make amends to people we have harmed we are beginning to interact with the world as spiritual warriors. Amend means to improve. While an apology and restitution to those we have harmed is worthy, our goal is to use our newfound knowledge of emptiness to create better relationships and a better world.

Methods of direct amends and how to discern making amends without causing additional harm are topics that are covered quite well in program literature. This writing is meant as a supplement to the Twelve Step program literature that is available. My hope in this chapter is to show how the activities of Step Nine and the intention behind the Steps are supporting our progression into spiritual warriors.

People that have worked the steps in the past and do a daily Tenth Step often find they have no direct amends to make when they get to Step Nine. This is normal. However, we may realize we still have deeper work to do. We may need to let go of resentments, forgive people we have judged wrong, and correct destructive thought patterns. In the end, we may find our greatest amends is to ourselves for the habitual thoughts we have that destroy our peace of mind and block our happiness.

For the newcomer and veteran twelve-stepper alike, Step Eight begins the switch from spiritual development focused on ourselves to spiritual development focused on our world. In Step Eight we began to cultivate our development of bodhichitta, the wish to end everyone's suffering. Step Nine begins our service to our fellow beings and the world. In this step we look ahead to the mindset and activities of a bodhisattva, a person that has realized bodhichitta. Even if we have not completely realized bodhichitta, we can begin to approximate the ideals of the way of the spiritual warrior.

The Way of the Bodhisattva

One becomes a bodhisattva when one has generated the mind of enlightenment. This is the mind that wishes each and every being pass completely beyond sorrow and suffering. A bodhisattva holds in their mind and heart bodhichitta at all times. This is a passive process, not an active one. True bodhichitta is imprinted on one's mind like a tattoo and cannot be lost. One way of achieving bodhichitta is presented in Step Eight. It is easier said than done and considered a very high state of being. After one realizes this enlightened mind, there are ten bodhisattva levels before total enlightenment is reached.

Despite the incredible achievement of realizing bodhichitta, a new bodhisattva has not even reached the first bodhisattva level! The first bodhisattva level is reached when the person with bodhichitta has the direct experience of emptiness or no-self during deep meditation. After this experience, the person knows without a doubt the exact nature of all phenomenon and realizes that personal "selves" do not exist. This experience marks the beginning of the first bodhisattva level and the path of habituation. Over the course of the next bodhisattva levels one begins to practice the Six Perfections which are covered in the chapter on Step Ten.

When the Buddha was asked how a bodhisattva should act, he gave the teaching which is known as the Diamond Cutter Sutra. In the Diamond Cutter Sutra the Buddha emphasizes it is critical to act in accordance with an understanding that nothing exists independent of our projections and naming. Indeed it is our projections that cause things to exist at all.

The Diamond Cutter Sutra is addressed to an advanced group of spiritual warriors and the instructions may be a bit concise for those of us that have not had a direct perception of no-self, but it is worth taking a look at. Even if you do not quite understand it, read along because it is considered a great blessing to do so according to the Buddha himself. This is the reason I have included this material. It plants positive seeds for enlightenment.

The Buddha's discourse begins like this:

> Subhuti, here, one who has correctly entered the bodhisattva's vehicle should generate the mind [of enlightenment] thinking this: 'As many as are included in the category of sentient being – born from egg, born from the womb, born from heat and moisture, born miraculously; with form, without form,

with discrimination, without discrimination, without discrimination but not without [subtle] discrimination – the realm of sentient beings, as many as are designated by imputation as sentient beings, all those I shall cause to pass completely beyond sorrow into the realm of nirvana without remainder of the aggregates. Although limitless sentient beings have thus been caused to pass completely beyond sorrow, no sentient being whatsoever has been caused to pass completely beyond sorrow.

What? Never mind all the different types of sentient beings. Read that last line again. The Buddha seems to contradict himself. First he says that limitless beings have become enlightened, and then he says no being whatsoever has become enlightened. Seems a bit odd. Subhuti, however, has no problem understanding what the Buddha is talking about. He understands because he has been listening to his teacher for years and following the path for years. The question remains for us, "What does he mean?"

The simplest explanation is that in the first instance he is referring to deceptive reality and in the second instance he is referring to ultimate reality. In the conventional way we view things, many sentient beings have followed the path that ends in enlightenment. However, from the view point of ultimate reality, there is no such thing as an independently living "sentient being" much less a "path to enlightenment". If the beings do not ultimately exist, then none of them could have been around to reach enlightenment.

> A **sentient being** is any living thing that has awareness or consciousness.

The Buddha continues explaining why a bodhisattva must simultaneously think "I'm going to bring sentient beings to enlightenment" and "No being has ever reached enlightenment nor ever will".

> Why is that? Subhuti, because if a bodhisattva engages in discriminating a sentient being, he is not to be called a 'bodhisattva.' Why is that? Subhuti, if anyone engages in discriminating a sentient being, or engages in discriminating a living being, or engages in discriminating a person, they are not to be called a 'bodhisattva'.

The Buddha is using the word "discriminating" in this situation to describe the mental process by which we are able to tell the difference between two objects – for instance a red pen and a blue pen. In the Heart Sutra the word "perceptions" is used to describe the same mental process. Both translations fall short of what is meant. The process is subtly different from the standard use of both words. The Buddha is talking about the process by which we tell two things apart at the basic level of raw data. It is the process by which we can tell that one leaf on a plant is behind (or in front of) another leaf.

When the Buddha says that a bodhisattva does not discriminate, he is simply saying that a bodhisattva does not see things as separate. A bodhisattva understands that the separate beings she is seeing and experiencing in everyday life are not really separate from herself. Indeed, according to the Prasangika school of Buddhist thought (See Appendix 1 for the classification of the different schools of Buddhist thought.), they are dependent on her projections and naming.

At the first bodhisattva level, a bodhisattva has had the direct experience of ultimate reality. They know how things really exist, even though they spend their day-to-day life in a world where things appear to exist independently. At higher bodhisattva levels, bodhisattvas spend more and more time in ultimate reality. Buddhas abide in ultimate reality but at the same time are cognizant of deceptive reality.

In the next paragraph the Buddha begins to talk about the First Perfection – that is the Perfection of Giving. The Perfection of Giving is the primary task of a bodhisattva at the first bodhisattva level.

> Further, Subhuti, a bodhisattva gives a gift without abiding in a thing; gives a gift without abiding in any phenomenon whatsoever. A gift should be given not abiding in visual form, nor should a gift be given abiding in sound, smell, taste, tactility, or a phenomenon. Subhuti, without abiding in discriminating anything whatsoever as any sign, thus does a bodhisattva give a gift.

In other words, the Perfection of Giving is realized, in part, when a bodhisattva is able to give a gift while understanding the emptiness of the giver, the emptiness of the gift and the emptiness of the person receiving the gift. A bodhisattva gives a gift without discriminating. They understand that there is no separate nature to the object or the people involved.

The Buddha in the Diamond Cutter Sutra continues to explain what it is to be a bodhisattva. Actually, there is not a lot of explanation and he does not deviate from his central idea. Again and again, he emphasizes that a bodhisattva is someone that understands the emptiness of all phenomenon. He repeatedly states that only by naming things do they exist.

He also describes repeatedly what tremendous merit it is to read even four lines of this sutra, study them, understand them and explain them to others. The Buddha claims the merit is greater than the pile of jewels and precious things that would fit into world systems equivalent in number to the number of grains of sand in the Ganges River times that number again. I think we are safe to assume from his description that the merit is greater than anything imaginable. This is good news, since a pile of merit even larger than that is needed to propel oneself to Buddhahood.

Unfortunately, the Buddha also says that anyone that reads, studies and understands the sutra will suffer tremendously. His exact words are

...they will be tormented; will be intensely tormented.

"Tormented" does not sound like much fun. Besides, were we not just told that the study of this teaching is an incredible virtue? Have we stumbled onto another contradiction? Actually it is because the sutra is such a powerful antidote to negative past deeds that it can cause grief.

The power of this sutra for purifying previously committed non-virtuous actions is such that deeds that would have resulted in unimaginable suffering will ripen into lesser, but still unpleasant sufferings. For instance, the karma to be killed or tortured will be purified and may ripen instead as a bad headache or perhaps a small accident. The act of reading, studying and understanding the sutra leads to the acceleration of the purification process, which then leads to the achievement of enlightenment in one lifetime. Not a bad trade off.

Of course, remember that the virtue and the purification power do not really exist. They only exist if the correct causes and conditions are present. That is, if you are projecting them into existence.

Life as a Spiritual Warrior

The bodhisattva is someone that is living life firmly founded on correct view. They are focused on amending all their relationships and the world, for they realize that the world they are experiencing is the world of their own creation. This creation is not a conscious process, but a natural result of their past thoughts and actions.

The way we improve the world and our relationships is by living in a way that mirrors the world we want to be a part of. To continue to have our needs met and receive love and sustenance, we give to others love and sustenance. Our commitment to ethical living and the Ten Virtues ensures that our experiences and environment will be pleasant. As we practice letting go and not getting angry at others we will find the people around us are more flexible and less critical of us. We find that as we move forward our life may not be instantaneously changed, but when viewed in perspective it is certainly getting better and better.

Saint Catherine of Siena (1347-1380) says:

The path to heaven lies through heaven, and all the way to heaven is heaven.

This is a reminder to us that as we progress the effort we put in will come back to us manyfold. As we move towards total enlightenment (heaven), the way is truly heavenly. We will find that this new way of life is fulfilling, and we will begin to "crave" wholesome things instead of the things and activities that we used to crave that were ultimately detrimental to us.

The Four Powers- The Power of Antidote

We are now ready to put the final destructive blow on our past. Traditionally the power of antidote consists of undertaking one of five make-up activities: 1) studying emptiness, 2) reciting mantras or holy words, 3) making images of enlightened beings, 4) making offerings, or 5) prayer and recitations. The rationale for these was described briefly in Step Eight. The highest antidote we can undertake is the study of emptiness. To this end, we have read about correct view in this book in Step Six and have also heard about emptiness directly from the Buddha in the Heart Sutra and the Diamond Cutter Sutra.

Our study of emptiness makes us ready to take direct action in correcting our non-virtuous activities from the past. We proceed as bodhisattvas when we can make amends without "discriminating" as directed by the Buddha in the Diamond Cutter Sutra. Not discriminating means to understand the emptiness of the amends, the person making the amends (ourselves) and the person the amends are directed at.

The following thoughts will help us approach our amends in a non-discriminating manner:

- The non-virtuous actions I did in the past will result in my future suffering if I do not completely destroy their seeds.

- I can completely destroy that unwanted karma by making appropriate amends.

- How I experience the person I am making amends to is dependent on my projections. They are not inherently bad or good. Their actions or words towards me are a result of my past deeds and are not necessarily "true" and certainly do not reflect on my value or my future. If I experience them as unpleasant, then the actions I am taking will result in their disappearance from my life. This will occur by either my perceptions of them changing or they will leave the circle of people I interact with.

- Myself and my amends do not exist independently. How I perceive these aspects of the amends process is also dependent on my projections which are based on previous thoughts and deeds. Neither I nor the amends I make are inherently good or bad. When it comes to making amends, my intention is everything. If the amends process upsets me or makes me feel happy, I have very little control over those reactions in the moment. My feelings and reactions are a result of my past actions and as I continue to develop spiritually my feeling and emotional reactions will continue to be more pleasing to me.

- The words and actions I use to make amends will plant new, positive potentials in my mind. Kind words will come back to me as kind words. This is how I am creating a joyous, happy and free life.

We are ready to make direct amends with these thoughts as our foundation. The complete destruction of negative karmic potentials will be the result of this final action in the sequence of the Four Powers.

Completing Step Nine

We complete Step Nine when we have made direct amends to the people on our Step Eight list wherever possible. If we have not finished the list due to some logistical problem, we do not let this hold ourselves back from moving forward. We trust that our intention to complete the amends will result in the opportunity to do so. Our amends may begin in Step Nine, but the actual work of amending our world and all our relationships is accomplished in the final three steps.

We move forward to Step Ten with a solid grasp of emptiness. We find that as a result of our Step Nine study we are more frequently applying correct view in our relations with others. We may have developed true bodhichitta, but even if we have not had that realization, we have a strong willingness to progress along a spiritual path.

In Step Ten, we will learn more about how to live the life we have chosen as a spiritual warrior. We also begin to learn the spiritual tasks, such as the Six Perfections, which each bodhisattva must master on the way to heaven. Turning our backs on the wreckage of our past and feeling secure in the knowledge that we have done our part to make amends we move forward to Step Ten.

STEP TEN
Continued to take personal inventory and when we were wrong promptly admitted it.

Diligent effort is needed to maintain a way of life that will lead to the end of all suffering. Our study of the preceding steps and inventory of our past actions and reactions gives us a good sense of our ideal way to live. However, it often seems like there is a gap between knowing what is right action and doing what is right. We continue to shrink the gap with Step Ten. We no longer are waiting to take inventory, but attempt to monitor ourselves at all times, admit when we get off track, and take corrective action.

Full Awareness or Mindfulness

In order to successfully catch ourselves in the act of getting off track, we need to develop an indispensible tool. This tool we are cultivating is **awareness**. To succeed in getting out of suffering, we need both introspective awareness and extrospective awareness.

Introspective awareness keeps a tab on our thoughts and feelings. It is essential for knowing what is motivating us. With a well developed introspective awareness, we can ward off actions we may regret and can redirect harmful thoughts to ones that are more enlightening. Even actions that cause no immediate harm do not serve us if they are motivated by ill-will or undertaken when we are angry, jealous or under the influence of similar negative emotions. Introspective awareness watches the door of body and speech and keeps us karmically safe.

Extrospective awareness, being aware of what is happening outside of ourselves, allows us to see the impact our actions or inactions have on the world. Even with the best of intentions, sometimes people and things get hurt. When we are mindful of how things turn out, we can evaluate our actions and make corrections if doing so seems prudent. In addition, extrospective awareness can also illuminate our internal state when introspective awareness fails. We may notice ourselves doing or saying things that do not ultimately serve us and realize they are motivated by a negative internal state.

Mindfulness is another term to describe the awareness we are talking about. I prefer the term awareness simply because the word implies action to me. With awareness, first we take notice and then we take action. For instance, we raise awareness about an issue, not just so people will know about it, but so they will take action. The term mindfulness seems to be used most often these days as if it is an end in itself. I hear people talk of practicing mindfulness, but I never hear what they do after they are mindful. Our intention is to use awareness or mindfulness to guard our treasure – our spiritual commitments. Master Shantideva in the *Guide to the Bodhisattva's Way of Life* emphasizes the necessity of developing introspective awareness:

> Those who wish to make progress on the spiritual path should
> be very attentive in guarding their minds. For if they do not
> practice guarding the mind, they will not be able to complete
> the path.

Being aware of what is going on in the mind and guarding it are essential. In Step Ten, we are continuing to take personal inventory and taking action on what we find. Personal awareness is key, but we also need to know what we want in our mind and what we are trying to eliminate.

The Buddha summarized 84,000 possible non-virtuous thoughts and actions as the Ten Misdeeds that were introduced in Step Four. Engaging in any of those would be a "wrong" to be identified in Step Ten. We can also use this step to keep ourselves out of danger in a more positive way by focusing on doing the Ten Virtues. If this is our focus, we do a "wrong" anytime we stray from our positive intention.

If we find ourselves busy with idle chatter or some other self-damaging behavior, we will want to correct this promptly. Most often, when we catch ourselves in the act, all that is needed is a simple course correction. We stop what we do not want to be doing and start what we want to be doing. If our watchfulness is lax and we do not realize our mistake until later, perhaps at the end of the day, we will want to clean up our act directly using the Four Powers.

It is not unusual to be caught up in the flow of circumstances and not realize until later that we were unnecessarily rude to someone or that withholding information on that application was a form of both lying and stealing. We find that as we continue practicing awareness of what we want to keep and what we want to give up, we will get quicker at catching ourselves straying from the path. With the passing of time, it will be easier for us to stay in integrity and treat people kindly and ethically.

The Four Forces or Four Powers

If you have been in program a while and completing a regular Tenth Step, you probably have been informally doing the Four Powers for years. They are a natural development of a spiritual way of living. See if you can recognize your own process in the following description.

First, the order in which we undertake the Four Powers does not matter, although there does seem to be a natural flow to them in practice. Regardless of the order, the completion of the practice results in the purification of negative karma. Ideally, we cut the negative karmic seed at the root with this practice and prevent the seed from ripening. These four forces follow the same principles as embodied by steps Three though Nine.

It is said that the four practices may reduce the intensity of karmic ripening but not completely eliminate the result in some cases. For instance, a deed that would result in our death or serious illness could be reduced to a minor ache instead. The effectiveness of the method depends on our motivation and dedication.

The **foundation power** is refuge itself. Here, we come back to our foundation. Traditionally, foundation power would be reaffirming refuge in the Three Jewels and reaffirming bodhichitta. There are many ways of meeting this objective. For the twelve-stepper this is akin to reaffirming our commitment by reviewing the insights gained and decisions made when we took the first three steps. We may specifically consider our goals, whether they be to avoid our drug of choice, be an effective sponsor or friend, or to reach full enlightenment for the benefit of others (bodhichitta).

A critical aspect of clearing the karma from non-virtuous thoughts and actions is knowing how they do not serve us and how they will result in future unpleasantness. This is the basis of the **power of destruction.** Destruction power is simply recognizing that what we did will come back to harm us and wishing we would not have done it. This is referred to as intelligent regret. It is not a long emotional process of guilt, worry or fear. It is like stepping into a puddle with open-toed shoes and exclaiming, "Oh, darn!" In that moment, you recognize that you made a wrong move and regret it.

The power of destruction is characterized by a simple acceptance of what has occurred. It requires letting go of the circumstances around the event. In our puddle example, perhaps we were preoccupied by an argument we just had or were in a hurry. It would be easy to think of other people to blame for our unhappy situation; perhaps someone distracted us. Here, we let go of all of that and simply accept that the situation and what we did were a result of prior causes and conditions that we were unable to control in the present moment.

We may take a moment to consider the situation, but we do not dwell in the past in a futile attempt to fix it or to figure out how to prevent it from ever happening again in a conventional way. If we find that we are dwelling on the situation, or rehashing it over and over, it is best to find people to talk to about it. Discussing the situation with someone else and admitting to them what we did wrong (confessing) helps to diffuse the emotional impact of the event and allow us to move forward in a positive manner. Indeed, "confession" is considered a vital part of the power of destruction and the practice of admitting our faults to another is the main topic and practice of Step Five.

After we have done something we regret, it is only natural to decide to not do it again. This is the **power of stopping, or restraint**. We resolve to restrain from this particular action or thought pattern. The strength of our resolution will help to destroy the potency of the karmic seed we have just planted, especially if we are able to succeed in not breaking our commitment to stop future actions of the same type.

If a behavior or thought is particularly difficult for us to control, we set a time frame. Perhaps we are enraged by another's behavior and, try as we might, we continue to have thoughts of malice and anger about this person. Setting a time frame of five minutes or even less may be prudent. We want to form a resolution to stop our harmful actions (remember harming others is ultimately more harmful to ourselves), and apply vigorous effort to keep our commitment. Further, we are looking to develop along spiritual lines, and as such we want to set clear but attainable goals. This willingness to restrain ourselves and take effort to develop along spiritual lines is the work of Step Six and Step Seven. In those steps, we turn our back on our character traits that do not serve us and make a resolution to live free of old baggage.

The final power is the **power of the antidote**. This is where the full force of destruction occurs. The poison was thinking and acting in a way that will result in the creation of a time bomb that, when detonated, will result in our unhappiness.

How do we defuse the bomb? What is the antidote for the poison?

The medicine we need is a deep understanding of emptiness and how the world really works. Further, we need to do everything we can to correct what we have done. If we spoke harshly to someone, we should follow up with an apology and kind words. If we stole, we need to make restitution if possible. Where we harmed life, we need to do what we can to undo the harm and make efforts to protect life in the future.

Although this description of the Four Powers is lengthy, it does not need to take much time to complete in practice. In real time, the recognition of a "misdeed" and a desire to make it right can take an instant. Directly apologizing or correcting our mistake may take a bit longer, but setting the intention to do so can also be instantaneous. The good news is that after we do this for awhile, the power of our introspective awareness increases. We catch ourselves and make a course correction before we have completed an action that will harm us. This development of awareness happens, in part, because we develop an aversion to the work of following up with people to make amends.

Practices that Help Develop Awareness

Awareness is a critical component of being able to progress on a spiritual path. We must be aware of what we are doing in order to ensure we stay on our path. Ultimately we need to be able to catch ourselves in the moment *before* we transgress our personal spiritual ideals. This certainly is a worthy lifetime goal, but where do we start?

The best way to begin developing awareness is to schedule a specific time to inventory our thoughts and behaviors each day. It is helpful to have a list of questions or the Ten Misdeeds/Ten Virtues to guide the inventory. Keep in mind as well, any specific character trait you are trying to cultivate or eliminate.

Here are some questions that are useful (from *Alcoholics Anonymous Big Book*, Fourth Edition, page 86):

- Were we resentful, selfish, dishonest or afraid?

- Do we owe an apology?

- Have we kept something to ourselves that should be discussed with another person at once?

- Were we kind and loving toward all?

- What could we have done better?

- Were we thinking of ourselves most of the time? Or were we thinking of what we could do for others, of what we could pack into the stream of life?

In one of the Buddhist traditions I trained in, the spiritual practitioners stop six times a day to check their behavior against their spiritual commitments. They record their findings in a notebook. This practice is called "keeping a book", and represents a high level commitment to ending all suffering.

The practitioner does not check every commitment each time, they rotate through their list. A beginner might be checking the Ten Virtues, while a monk or nun would have hundreds of separate commitments (vows) to check. The person with just ten would do six today and then the last four tomorrow and then start over with the first two on the list. They would continuously rotate through the list over and over.

This method is extremely effective at increasing awareness. The inventory makes us more aware of what we have been doing. Even more valuable is the continuous review of what we want in our life. Bringing our intentions to our mind frequently increases our awareness of our objectives in each moment. This awareness increases our ability to act in accordance with our ideals and attracts more goodness into our life. That is in accordance with the law of cause and effect and the law of attraction.

In Twelve Step circles, it is more common for people to undertake the review once a day, often in the evening. Even this may be ambitious for many of us. When I first started in Twelve Step programs I was unable to do anything regularly once a day. My first major victory was reading the daily reader once a day, which I achieved after quite a few years in program. It was about a decade more before I was able to do a daily written Tenth Step.

Even if we are not writing our inventory out, we can still be taking an inventory in our mind. The more effort we put into developing awareness, and a written inventory helps with this, the faster our progress will be. However, even if all we can muster is the willingness to take inventory, we will still progress. Our intention to progress along spiritual lines creates the karmic seeds for the desire to grow spiritually to increase. In addition, we also gain the ability to accomplish things we never dreamed we would be able to accomplish.

The Six Perfections

The Tenth Step for a bodhisattva is focused on cultivating virtue. The bodhisattva is intent on reaching total enlightenment for the sake of all beings. The cause of such a miraculous transformation involves accumulating a great deal of merit. This merit is the result of certain actions. Fortunately, we are given a guide as to what to do. This guide is in the form of the Six Perfections. The Six Perfections are:

- The Perfection of Giving

- The Perfection of Ethical Living

- The Perfection of Not Getting Angry
- The Perfection of Joyful Effort
- The Perfection of Concentration
- The Perfection of Wisdom

Each perfection is a primary task of each of the first six bodhisattva levels. The task of the first level is the Perfection of Giving. The task for the second level is the Perfection of Ethical Living, and so on. Acting from an understanding of correct world view, a bodhisattva progresses along the path to enlightenment by practicing the Six Perfections. While we can certainly work on each of the perfections simultaneously, there is a rationale for the order.

The Perfection of Giving

It seems to me that the Perfection of Ethical Living should come before all others. Is not living morally the foundation of every spiritual path? But instead we find the Perfection of Giving is the first task. As it turns out, the rationale behind this is sensible and simple.

When we carefully examine the motivation behind each of our non-virtuous actions, we frequently find fear at the bottom. We steal because we ultimately fear we will not have enough. We lie to protect our image or assets. We focus on others' deficiencies in gossip or to discredit them, all so that we will look better and be more secure in our position.

In each case we are scared of losing something or of not having enough. The antidote to this fear is getting to a place where we can effortlessly give away everything we have without regret, remorse, or even a sense of loss. This is the Perfection of Giving.

Master Shantideva guides us on how to proceed:

> At the beginning the Guide directs us to acts of charity such as giving vegetables and the like. Once we have grown accustomed to these, then gradually, in good time, we find we can offer even our flesh.

The idea of giving whatever we have without a thought is well beyond most of our capabilities, but that is not where we start. We start small in our practice of generosity by giving small things like food. As our understanding of emptiness progresses and as we find that this world view is working for us, we naturally expand our generosity.

In our spiritual practice we are cautioned to never work beyond our capacity. Knowing our capacity is very important and not necessarily obvious. When it comes to generosity, working within our capacity means that we do not give unless the desire arises naturally in our hearts. To give to others because we think we ought to is actually a wrong view. It is based on a belief of scarcity. The idea that there is not enough for everybody and that unless we give up what we need others will go without is not correct view. We progress along our spiritual paths the fastest by showing *ourselves* the love of generosity first.

It is not that hard to determine one's natural capacity. Consider a homeless family. We may think nothing of giving them one dollar to help out. Now consider progressively greater generosity to see where we fall. How about five dollars or twenty dollars or one hundred or one thousand? What about having them over for dinner or to stay the night, or a week? Would you be willing to give them all your savings or your house? Perhaps we found ourselves comfortable with giving twenty dollars and a ride to the local shelter. This is our capacity. Our capacity will change as we progress, just as Master Shantideva foretells.

The Perfection of Ethical Living

The Perfection of Ethical Living is the main practice of the Tenth Step. There is not much more to say about this since we have covered it in detail throughout this step and in Step Four as well. The main aspect of moral living is avoidance of the Ten Misdeeds: harming others, stealing, sexual misconduct, lying, using harsh words, engaging in meaningless or divisive talk, coveting what other people have, wishing ill upon others, and holding wrong world view. For Buddhists with specific vows or pledges, ethical living includes upholding these as well.

The Perfection of Not Getting Angry

Once we are living consistently in an ethical manner, we may still find we are haunted by mental afflictions like jealousy, fear and anger. Fortunately, these are getting less and less due to our understanding of how the world works. We now know that whenever we have a mental affliction, not only is it focused on the gakja (something that does not exist), it is founded on wrong view. Understanding such as this is helping us crush our mental afflictions.

Getting rid of the mental affliction of anger is the task of the Third Perfection. Anger is singled out because it certainly is one of the major unpleasant mental afflictions. It manifests in many forms: frustration, irritability, rage, resentment and annoyance. Anger can destroy friendships, relationships, careers, and our own peace of mind.

Similar to our approach in the Perfection of Giving, we start out small and progress. For instance, we might be able to eliminate angry outbursts long before we are able to eliminate our internal anger reactions. We may learn to tolerate minor inconveniences and discomfort before we can accept major transgressions and setbacks. The Perfection of Anger occurs when the seeds for anger are destroyed and we never have an internal angry reaction again.

When I went through the angry period in my life I learned that I could not control the spark of anger, but I could douse the fire of anger by reframing situations and by refusing to think the thoughts that would feed the flames. I thought that I could end all my anger by this process alone. As it turns out, the only way to kill the spark of anger is to realize, one hundred percent, the emptiness of the world. The direct experience of ultimate reality is the true antidote for anger.

In the meantime, we still can progress in our practice of not getting angry. As Master Shantideva tells us:

> If there is something you can do about it, why get upset? If there is nothing you can do about it, what's the use in getting upset?

This is actually quite similar to our own Serenity Prayer:

> Grant me the serenity to accept the things I cannot change, the courage to change the things I can, and the wisdom to know the difference.

We see that acceptance is truly the key to destroying anger. Anger arises in two instances. One is when we do not accept what is beyond our control and not to our liking. The other is when we are not taking care of ourselves and are blaming that on others.

For instance, we walk into the house tired and become angry at whoever is there (our children, housemates or partner) for not doing the dishes or something of the sort. The anger arises because we are tired and the tiredness may be coming from overcommitting ourselves. In this sense, the anger comes from not taking care of ourselves.

In addition, why get upset if there is something we can do about it? A simple request for the dishes to be done could be all that is required. And if we believe that "they should know" and already have them done, then we have just slipped into believing that we can control something we are powerless over. We have slipped into non-acceptance.

The following excerpt on acceptance, adapted from *Alcoholics Anonymous Big Book* (Fourth edition, page 417), tells us:

> Acceptance is the answer to all my problems today. When I am disturbed, it is because I find some person, place, thing, or

situation – some fact of my life – unacceptable to me, and I can find no serenity until I accept that person, place, thing, or situation as being exactly the way it is supposed to be at this moment. Nothing, absolutely nothing, happens… by mistake.

That pretty well sums up a way of thinking and living that will bring us to ultimate peace.

Perfection of Joyful Effort

This next perfection is usually called the Perfection of Effort, but the translation of the word effort is not quite right. This perfection is actually about taking joy in doing good. When you are taking joy in doing good and other people see you, they might comment on how much effort you are putting into helping people. From the outside it looks like effort, but from the inside you just feel an abundance of energy coming from the joy of doing good things.

The many hours Mother Teresa spent at the bedside of people with leprosy and other afflictions could be seen as the Perfection of Effort. To the outside world, her life may look like sacrifice and tireless effort, but perhaps from her internal landscape, she was experiencing only the joy in doing good.

The Perfection of Joyful Effort follows naturally as we learn to accept life as it is. When we no longer experience frustration or a drain of energy from trying to get life to match our wishes, we are more open to the joy and peace in simple service. We give in the moment, whatever is needed, to whoever needs it. We do not need to force working on this perfection, since as our capacity increases, the Perfection of Joyful Effort follows automatically.

The Final Two Perfections

The final two perfections are the Perfection of Concentration and the Perfection of Wisdom. These two are the topic of Step Eleven. Meditative concentration is the tool we use to attain wisdom, and the tool we use to develop stable concentration is introspective awareness. In Step Ten, we are laying the foundation for development of strong concentration by cultivating introspective awareness and by our commitment to ethical living.

Yes, ethical living is an important basis for developing concentration. Meditative concentration is difficult to achieve if we are not living ethically. For instance, if we have had an argument or harmed someone in any way, as soon as we sit down to meditate, our feelings about the situation will arise. Likewise, our thoughts will be drawn to contemplating the situation. We may justify our actions by focusing on our reasons for acting as we did or we may worry about how we can make the situation better. In either case, these thoughts distract us from our meditative object.

Completing Step Ten

We continue to take personal inventory and make course corrections until we reach total enlightenment. The state of total enlightenment is also referred to as the "path of no more learning". At this level of spiritual development we have total omniscience. When one can "know" all things at all times, the need to take inventory falls away. This is something to look forward to. In the meantime, we move on to Step Eleven when we understand the rationale for Step Ten and have a plan for implementing the inventory process in our daily lives.

STEP ELEVEN
Sought through prayer and meditation to improve our awareness of ultimate reality and connection to our intuitive center, praying only for knowledge of right action and the power to carry that out.

The key to enlightenment is held in the last two perfections which are embodied in Step Eleven. In this step we seek to use prayer and meditation to guide us in right action and to eventually allow us to perceive ultimate reality (emptiness) directly. Meditation (the Fifth Perfection) is the cornerstone to all important realizations upon the path to enlightenment and is necessary for gaining wisdom (the Sixth Perfection).

The original wording of the step begins, "Sought through prayer and meditation to improve our conscious contact with God." When confronted with this statement I was initially at a loss. Since in this work we are purporting that there is no "God", at least not one with total power over the cosmos, I needed to adapt the step to embody the spiritual essence of the step without "God". What I realized was that it was hard for me to find an appropriate simple substitution since there are two actions that "conscious contact with God" represents.

The first action we need to replace is making conscious contact with God and learning to align ourselves with his will. Instead, for us, we are making conscious contact with a part of ourselves that has a deep connection to all that is. This part could be called our buddha nature, our higher self, our intuitive center, the Tao within, our natural center, love, or a piece of the source within. It is a part of us that knows right action and when we are connected to it we "do without doing and it all gets done". In Step Eleven, we are trying to increase our conscious contact with our true center so that life will become less strifeful and more effortless.

The second aspect referred to in making conscious contact with God is getting to know God better. In the traditional interpretation of the steps, God is our creator and it makes perfect sense that we would want a better relationship with this being. However, from our view, we are created by the marriage of emptiness and karma, and not by "God". What we are wanting to make "conscious contact" with is "our creator" – emptiness or ultimate reality.

However, we do not want to have *conscious* contact with ultimate reality. The life changing experience we are seeking occurs in deep meditation and in a state where all our faculties are shut down. Our senses and basic consciousness are at a standstill for the short period of time when we have our experience of ultimate reality, or emptiness, directly. Due to this, I changed the wording from "conscious contact" to "awareness of ultimate reality". Not only do we want to have this direct experience, which we certainly will be aware of, we want to increasingly improve our awareness of ultimate reality using meditation.

The Fifth Perfection

Perfect meditative concentration is one of the higher goals of Step Eleven. To reach this goal, we combine rock solid and stable concentration with fully-conscious mindful awareness. This perfected meditative state is referred to as quietude, shamata (in Sanskrit) or calm-abiding.

Shamata is defined as, "The single-mindedness which is imbued with the exceptional bliss of practiced ease due to single-pointed meditation on its object". In practice, this means the meditator can sit down, direct their attention at whatever object they choose, and effortlessly hold their attention on it with great clarity for any length of time. Their solid concentration allows them to stay fixed on the object, but they also have the ability to move from object to object with full conscious awareness and stable focus on each object.

Like anything one is good at, the trained meditator no longer has to think about what they are doing and instead has ease due to extensive practice. In meditation, this practiced ease leads to a blissful state of joy, equanimity and tranquility. For those of us that have found the initial stages of meditative practice difficult or uncomfortable, this promise of bliss is quite reassuring.

> **Shamata** is the single-mindedness which is imbued with the exceptional bliss of practiced ease due to single-pointed meditation on its object.

Long before we perfect concentration, we will find regular meditation a valuable practice in that it will calm our mind, help us connect to our center, and provide us with insights into ourselves, our reactions and the world. The Fifth Perfection of meditative concentration is not an end in itself. It is the tool to progress along the path to enlightenment and it is required for the direct experience of ultimate reality.

The Sixth Perfection

The Sixth Perfection is prajna paramita – the perfection of wisdom. In its perfect form, it is a state of abiding in ultimate reality at all times. An initial aspiration is to have the brief transient experience of ultimate reality from the platform of shamata. For this reason, the Sixth Perfection rides on the back of the Fifth Perfection. In order to experience emptiness directly, you must be able to rest effortlessly on your meditation object.

The transient experience of emptiness profoundly changes the practitioner. All your life you see things a certain way and the world seems to function a certain way. The way you see things conventionally is what we call deceptive reality. Then you hear that reality is ultimately not the way you think. If you trust the person that tells you your view is wrong, you may believe them, but it is not until you actually experience ultimate reality yourself that all doubts and a lifetime of experiences that support wrong view are erased. You still see the world the same way, but you do not believe that it really is as it seems. You will never think the old way about the world again. Because you finally know how the world works, you can align yourself with it. Once you have a hold on correct view, your days are numbered as a normal mortal.

It is like I tell you that I just bought a bunch of purple carrots. Well, you know that carrots are orange, so you are not sure what to think about my statement. Am I joking? All your life everyone said carrots were orange and all the carrots you saw were orange. Indeed, not until you actually see purple carrots will you be certain that they exist. Once you experience it directly, no one will be able to convince you otherwise. So it is with the direct perception of ultimate reality.

A person that has had the direct perception of emptiness, no-self, or ultimate reality (different words for the same experience) is called an arya. They are also referred to as stream-enterers. This is because after the experience they enter a stream that ends in enlightenment. It is like getting on a conveyer belt or Disney ride where the final destination is enlightenment. This experience assures that the final goal will soon be reached, because the arya now really knows how the world works and they can start behaving in a way that works with ultimate reality and not against it.

Meditation Practice

How does one cultivate such exceptional concentration as described in the Fifth Perfection? The methods for developing concentration vary, but the basic instruction is: get into a comfortable position that will foster your alertness, close your eyes, pick an object to focus on and then hold your attention on it. Each time you become aware that your attention is no longer on the object, gently return your focus back to the object.

Good luck!

Initially, most of us find that we spend much more time off the object than focused on the object. It is wise to not get upset at the wandering mind. Since it is the natural tendency of the mind to wander, when we catch ourselves off the object we want to rejoice in the fact we have caught ourselves off the object. We also want to give positive reinforcement to the other natural tendency of the mind, which is to become aware that it has wandered. In this process we are training our mind in both concentration (focus) and introspective awareness (mindfulness).

This is the basic instruction, but there are many sources that offer further instruction. I refer you to *ACI Course Three: Applied Meditation* or the meditation book by Master Culadasa (John Yates) currently in press. You will find in these sources a variety of additional instruction. There are preliminary practices that will help set up the mind for a good meditation session, advice on how to select the ideal object to focus on (each teacher has their own opinion), and corrections to counteract the many obstacles that can arise to impede practice (like not wanting to meditate, monkey-mind, agitation, dullness, sleepiness and more).

The type of meditation I am describing here is meditation focused on cultivating calm-abiding. This is an essential goal, but not the only possible reason for meditating. Meditating reduces stress, contributes to a healthy hormone profile in the body, and increases well-being.

Beginning meditators are best off picking a form of meditation that will help them establish a regular practice. This is the first goal. Without regularity one cannot reap much benefit. To get a flavor of what serious meditation practice is like, I recommend a vipassana retreat with S.N. Goenka assistant teachers (dhamma.org). If that fuels your heart, keep it up – but if it does not thrill you, then follow your heart to a practice that resonates with you. Only you can know the best meditation practice for yourself. We always need to keep in mind to not get beyond our level and capacity. In Tai Chi, we have the seventy percent rule. We work at seventy percent capacity for the quickest progress.

At the beginning, you may find that guided meditations, visualizations, or reciting prayers or holy words suit you. Do whatever it takes to establish a regular practice. Once you get good at meditating, or acquire it as a habit, then regular practice becomes automatic. A couple of my favorite Step Eleven practices follow: 1) contemplation and 2) connecting with my "higher power" or intuitive center.

Contemplative Meditation

Contemplation, the action of thinking about something carefully, is a form of meditation sometimes referred to as analytical meditation. In this method one reads a spiritual passage, piece of program literature or pithy quote and then thinks about it.

I have used a variety of readings for this, but one favorite practice is to take the serenity prayer and go through it word by word. I start with "Grant" and think about what that means. Then I move onto "me" and consider what that means and what it means when combined with "grant". When I slowly digest each word, I see how my body reacts and how it makes me feel. Is it upsetting or is it calming? Do I like it or not?

> Grant me the serenity to accept the things I cannot change,
> the courage to change the things I can,
> and the wisdom to know the difference.

Another favorite contemplation is to take the acronym **ODAT** (One Day At a Time) and apply the alternate words: Opportunity Desire Ability Time. I use this to decide if something is truly right action for me today. I consider my situation using the following questions:

- Is there an **Opportunity**?

- Do I have the **Desire**?

- Do I have the **Ability**?

- Do I have the **Time**?

Let's say someone has asked me to go to the fair with them. My answer to the first question would be "Yes," there is an opportunity – someone has invited me. The answer to the second question I may know immediately, or I may need to get quiet and check with my heart. When I am quiet, I may learn that I would like to go with the person somewhere, but I do not really want to go to the fair. This insight allows me to form my response to them. If I am not sick and can walk around, then I am able to go to the fair and can answer yes to the third question. If I have no homework, housework, appointments, or other obligations then I have the time and can answer affirmative to the last question.

Contemplation helps us establish conscious contact with our intuitive center, an important goal of Step Eleven. It also helps calm and focus the mind and can lead to intuitive insights with profound impact. In addition, if practiced regularly, contemplative meditation helps set the stage for more advanced meditative training.

Connecting to Our Intuitive Center

Long before I studied Buddhism or meditation I was confronted with Step Eleven: "Sought through prayer and meditation to improve our conscious contact with our higher power..." I had heard the Buddha had become enlightened by focusing his attention on his body. I did not have a clue what enlightenment was nor did I know who the Buddha was. I vaguely understood he was some great spiritual guy and that enlightenment was some desirable state. So when I sat down to meditate for the first time, I focused my attention on my body. If it was good enough for the Buddha, it was good enough for me.

Sitting on the couch, I sought to connect to my higher power. I kept awareness on my body in general and tried to focus my attention specifically on my tantien (dantian). The center of the tantien lies about two finger widths below the navel and is in the center of the body.

I knew from my practice of internal arts (Chi gung and Tai chi) that the tantien is considered the center of life force energy in the body. Indeed, someone that is in perfect harmony with all-that-is is said to move and act from their tantien. The converse is also true. Someone that is moving and acting from their center is in perfect harmony with all-that-is.

Many of the same attributes ascribed to someone acting in accordance with God's will are also true of the "God-less" person acting from their center. People say it is "God's will" if the doors open and things go well. Likewise, a person moving from their center finds their actions become effortless, automatic and successful. And both the person connected to God or the person connected to their intuitive center find that they get intuitive ideas on how to proceed or when to stop moving forward with a particular course of action. When things do not go according to their wishes, both the person connected to God as well as the person connected to their center take it in stride and without a lot of anguish.

It is possible that people that think they are connecting with God are really connecting with their intuitive center or vice versa. In fact, the best account of the path to enlightenment I have ever read was written by Bernadette Roberts, a Christian contemplative. It is clear in her account what we call the direct experience of ultimate reality she considers a direct contact with God upon the "self" falling away.

She uses the similar words to describe the experience as Buddhists do: "no-self, black hole, darkness, nothingness". She, however, believes that this emptiness of the self allows for a direct look at God without the filter of the self and that the "darkness is due to a superabundance of light – like being struck blind when looking directly at the sun".

God, emptiness – call it whatever. The end result of the experience is a transformation that ends in enlightenment. For more of Bernadette Roberts' journey, I recommend *The Path to No-Self*. It is a little hard to read since she is trying to describe something outside of most of our experiences, but worthwhile. It is interesting to note that when she describes the end of the path, she no longer refers to God, but to all that Is.

Necessary steps along the path is the destruction of both personal "self" and God as a "self" or God as a being. Indeed, at the end of Bernadette's path, she says that she needed to acclimate to a "life without an ultimate reality", suggesting that pretty much everything falls away to leave only Truth. A truth that can only be lived in and experienced directly. I suppose we will learn what that is when we get there.

In the meantime, back on my couch, I would focus on my center and listen for a desire in my heart. Not the desires of craving or addiction, but a sweet childlike lifting of my spirits and the heart's movement towards something. I was told when I first started the program that the desire to do something was one of the ways my higher power let me know its will for me.

In my early days, I was frequently depressed, so often times I received no special message and felt no desire to do anything in particular. Most often I left the couch without inspiration, but with resolve to do the next right thing. Since nothing special was required of me, I would turn to the chores.

Another gem I received early on my path was from my spiritual mentor in program. She told me that love is the strongest force in the universe and that self-love is the fast track to recovery. "Fast" is something I am attracted to, especially when it means leaving my suffering behind. So on my couch, and in my suffering, I would look for my heart's desire. I would ask myself, "What is the most loving and kind thing I can do for myself today?" and then I would act on the answer. Sometimes, even when I could think of nothing special to do to take care of myself, just the fact I had asked and was willing to act in my own behalf soothed my broken heart.

...and the Power to Carry It Out

Once we have an idea what action would be in alignment with our center and heart, we move forward into action. This is the acid test. If we are connected to our center and are able to move and accomplish something, then it is certainly right action. However, if we take action and are unable to accomplish our goal, is it still right action?

I believe there are times when our part is to take action regardless of outcome. If we have prayed and connected to our center, and also have the power to do our part, then we are acting in alignment with right action. Other times, we may notice that we thought we had enough clarity of right action to proceed, but the results surprised us. Reviewing such a situation will provide us insight into whether our alignment with right action was truly in place when we moved into action.

I learned to do my "higher power's will" or take right action by noticing the different results between when I was taking action that I felt was one hundred percent right and when I thought the action might not be completely right. From reviewing my motivation and the results, I learned to trust my intuitive sense. I learned that most of the time my intuition was correct, however, sometimes I went astray. This was usually because sometimes I was unable to let go of something that was impeding my ability to take right action.

For instance, in 2006, I lost a job I loved. After a few hopeful job prospects fell flat, I got the sense that applying would not make a difference. I did not think I would be getting a job soon. Still, I continued to go ahead and look for work anyway. After all, I was unemployed, had a family and a house payment. I thought I had to look for a job or otherwise I would be irresponsible. I did this for months, even though I had the intuitive sense that I was not going to get a job and could use my time better in a different way.

I finally let go of my desire to find a job and used the time to write my first book, *The Answers Are Within – A collection of personal stories*. After the book was completed, I worked a number of part-time positions until I found my way to the high desert of Arizona where I spent a couple years meditating, healing from the surfacing repressed memories of my childhood, studying the Buddhist tradition, and finally writing this treatise.

In this situation, my intuition told me that looking for a job through the usual channels was not right action. Supporting this realization was the fact that when I ignored my gut "knowing" and pushed on to look for work, I did not have the "power" to make a job happen. Indeed, since it was not right action for me at the time, it became increasingly harder to keep up the effort. In the end, I was not given the power to even continue looking for a job.

When I gave up my fruitless effort to find a job I found more peace, although I still had some fear and some reservations that I was being irresponsible. These residual minor mental afflictions are not "bad" and I am not "bad" for having them, they simply reflect my spiritual capacity at the time. We can all look forward to such mental afflictions being eventually eliminated as we progress along the path. Not by direct effort or repression, but as a natural outcome of our efforts to study emptiness, mediate and stay connected to our center. As we learned in Step Seven, these shortcomings cannot be relieved directly, but our dedication to the path sets us up for success.

Completing Step Eleven

We continue to deepen our connection to our source and seek to experience ultimate reality until we reach total enlightenment. We realize that experiencing emptiness or the reality of no-self directly is a high priority. We understand that experience will move us into a stream that ends in enlightenment. As guided by our intuitive center, we undertake the next right action needed to move us closer to that goal. Although the experience of emptiness is a high priority, and we hold our intention as such, we trust our process. Acting in alignment with our center will move us towards our intention, although the outcome may not be obvious from our current vantage point.

We are ready to move on to Step Twelve once we have learned our way of making contact with our inner center and have established a regular practice of staying connected. We continue learning more about this connection and how to know what right action is, what obstacles block us, and how to realize the power to undertake right action. We learn by listening for intuitive messages, acting on those messages and observing the results. We remain mindful of our feelings, actions and reactions and use our awareness to inform our decision on how to proceed to act in ways that are truly in alignment with our highest and best interests.

STEP TWELVE
Having had a spiritual awakening as a result of these steps, we tried to carry this message to others and to practice these principles in all areas of our lives.

Once the Buddha became enlightened, he taught his method for forty-five years and guided many people – some to enlightenment and others to more mundane levels of joy and peace. We, too, have achieved a spiritual awakening and continue with our bodhisattva activities by doing service, teaching what we have learned (the Dharma), and helping others. These are the activities that lead to total enlightenment.

The Perfection of Giving

The Perfection of Giving was first discussed in Step Ten as the task of the first bodhisattva level. When we get to Step Twelve, we find that what we have learned and our spiritual progress puts us in a position to truly be useful to all others. It is now that we can take our giving to a new level.

The practice of generosity can be divided into four components:

1. Giving material objects

2. Giving protection or freedom from fear

3. Giving affection, love and care

4. Giving spiritual teachings and guidance

The last three components of this Perfection are all important aspects of our Twelfth Step work. When we work with others and share what we have learned and our experiences walking the path, we are helping people move out of fear (component two), we are giving love and caring (component three), and we are teaching the dharma (component four).

When we get to Step Twelve, we have achieved a new understanding of how the world works, have greater clarity and know greater personal peace. We notice that the people around us are struggling in the same ways we used to. We naturally want to help them. Along with this desire to help, we now have more energy (power) to do so because we are no longer wasting our energy on unproductive thinking and activities.

> A Twelve Step Fellowship is a "high object" to give money to (see potency chart in Step Four) because they are in the position to help a great number of people in need. **If you are struggling financially, giving more, not less, is the key to financial abundance.** That is the law of cause and effect (karma).

We once again find that when we reach a step after completing the preceding steps, it almost naturally starts happening in our life. As we come upon Step Twelve, we have let go of old useless habits and are naturally attracted to doing good and giving the highest thing we can give – freedom from suffering.

People may be attracted to the changes in us and interested in learning what we are doing differently, but not everyone is ready to hear about "how karma works" and how their "bad" boss or relative is really coming from themselves. As Mahatma Ghandi said:

> There are people in the world so hungry, that God cannot appear to them except in the form of bread.

In every instance, our intention is to give the highest form of assistance we can give. The greatest thing we can give anyone is teachings on how to end their own suffering permanently. However, everyone is at a different place on the path and many people have other needs that are screaming for attention louder than self-actualization. We use our intuitive center to determine if the person in front of us just wants an ear so they can vent their frustration or if they are open to learning how to reframe their situation based on an admittance of powerlessness and knowledge of the emptiness of objects.

We let go of our own agenda for other people, trusting that they too have their own guidance center and are operating at their own level and personal capacity. Everyone grows at their own pace and in their own way. Our primary job is to keep in alignment with our source.

Although we are being encouraged to be generous, we do this thoughtfully. To give whatever is requested of us may not always be for the highest good of all concerned. We need to take care of ourselves and dependents first, ever expanding our circle of care. Sometimes it is wise to withhold giving material objects when to do so would enable someone to continue with self-destructive behavior (e.g. drug use). We check with our intuitive center to determine right action. Ultimately, we may find we give without trying to figure out what is best for the other person, allowing them complete responsibility for their own self-destruction or self-care. In this way, all vestiges of control are relinquished. We trust that as we give to the world, so it will give to us. This is the law of karma. In all situations, we search our feelings and motives when we are presented with an opportunity to give. We seek to be generous, but always to stay within our capacity to do so. In all situations, we stay connected to our center and trust that connection to guide our actions, for right action comes from the center.

Service – How it works

In Twelve Step circles it is said we cannot keep what we have received without giving it away. After our study of how karma and emptiness works, we understand even more the truth of this. If we want freedom from addiction, we must see ourselves helping others become free of theirs. Service is what we do to plant the mental potentials that create freedom from our addictions and ultimately from all suffering.

Service is a topic thoroughly described in the literature that accompanies each Twelve Step program. Anything that helps spread the message to the person that is still suffering is service. This includes working the steps, making outreach calls, attending a meeting, or taking a formal service position at the group level or higher. We consult our intuitive center before we agree to any service commitment, whether that be agreeing to sponsor someone, or serving as a group or intergroup leader.

One important note about service, in light of our Mahayana perspective, is that once one has achieved the wish to reach total enlightenment for the sake of all sentient beings, all activities of that person are considered service. The intention to serve all others makes getting up in the morning and brushing one's teeth a highly virtuous activity. Indeed, the interconnectedness of all life means that even if all I do is stay at home and work the steps to the best of my ability, I am being of service. This is true

Buddhism can be divided into two general traditions:

Mahayana is the path of seeking buddhahood for the sake of all beings.

Hinayana is the path to enlightenment for oneself.

regardless of my bodhisattva status. Although, we may tend to think of sponsoring or working directly with newcomers as the highest form of service in Twelve Step programs, the truth is that any effort we invest in self improvement and using the spiritual principles embodied by the Steps is a tremendous help to everyone. Practicing these principles in all areas of our lives is how we carry the message to others.

Completing Step Twelve

The nature of our spiritual awakening results in a perpetual desire to carry the message of how to end suffering to others. We move forward, continuing to do the next right thing, whether that be studying emptiness, taking right action in our relationships, cultivating full-minded

> Practicing the principles embodied in the Twelve Steps in all areas of our lives is how we carry the message to others.

awareness, deepening our meditation and connection to all that is, or serving others in the highest manner possible. Step Twelve reminds us to practice the principles embodied in all of the Steps for the rest of our days.

Summary of the Twelve Steps as a Path to Enlightenment

To reach the permanent cessation of all mental afflictions, a number of key realizations must be attained along the way. The Twelve Steps are a complete path to enlightenment and all one needs to reach a state of everlasting bliss. As we have moved through the Steps, we have completed the following spiritual milestones:

- renunciation
- refuge
- purification of obstacles
- understanding of correct world view
- development of bodhichitta
- attainment of meditative concentration
- a deepening connection to the source of all our good within us.

The first three steps represent a **renunciation** process. In them, we examine our old ways, renounce the ones that are not working for us, and decide to enter a spiritual path. In Step One, we admit our way of living life is not giving us the results we want. We explore all the ways that this world has covert and overt suffering to provide us

> **Renunciation** is letting go of all things that do not support achieving spiritual goals.

with motivation to leave our old life behind. In Step Two, we realize there might be a better way of living and learn about the law of cause and effect (karma). We conclude this new view could give us more satisfaction and ultimate peace. In Step Three, we decide to give living in alignment with this new world view a try. At this point, we take **refuge** in this new way of thinking and acting. We take refuge in the way of the buddhas.

Step Four begins our work to clear away the obstacles to peace, happiness and freedom. We make an inventory of our ethical and unethical behavior. We continue to strengthen our resolve to live ethically by exploring the more subtle aspects of the law of karma and how it works with emptiness in Step Five and Step Six. This study of **correct world view** strengthens our resolve to renounce our old ways and embrace a new manner of living which we then formally do in Step Seven.

We move into action as a bodhisattva by first studying what it means to be a bodhisattva and then how to gain **bodhichitta** in Step Eight and Step Nine. In steps Four through Nine, we destroy old, past karma and the method of **purification** we use is detailed in its entirety in Step Ten. In the last three steps, we undertake the activities of a bodhisattva by working on the Six Perfections. In particular, we focus on developing **meditative concentration** so that we may be able to directly experience ultimate reality. Our meditative practice also strengthens our connection to our intuitive center, allowing right action to easily flow through us.

Until we reach buddhahood, we continue to use the Twelve Steps as a guide along our way. In many Buddhist traditions, a personal teacher is the key to reaching enlightenment. I have found that my path does not include a spiritual guide that I live close to and consult daily. Without a human teacher, my guide and refuge has become the Twelve Steps themselves. I rely on the Twelve Steps, my intention to reach enlightenment for the service of all others, and my connection to my center to lead me along the path.

CONCLUSION

This treatise is meant to be suggestive only. There is more than one path to enlightenment. I hope that you find something in this work helpful. Certainly, discard anything you find limiting or that insults your intellect. Even if the model I presented is inaccurate or limiting, it may still be quite useful. If you follow the suggestions in this book, your life will improve, and when the usefulness of the model no longer serves you, a better model will present itself. This work is meant to supplement program literature, not supplant it.

The answers are within each of us and will be revealed to us as we move forward on our paths. As we keep our house in order and act as spiritual warriors, great things will come to pass. We give love, caring, guidance and receive the same in kind. Where once there was only wreckage and suffering, now there is beauty, peace and grace. Our connection to our center provides us with the guidance needed to live our days in a manner that is beyond our wildest pre-program dreams.

Let us go forth and spread goodness everywhere. Ultimately, we are all connected and joined. We create each other in some mysterious way, and it is my hope to recreate all of us as happy, joyous and free.

Would all who care to join me in closing with the Serenity Prayer?

Grant me the serenity to accept the things I cannot change, the courage to change the things I can, and the wisdom to know the difference.

TO THE PERSON THAT BELIEVES IN GOD

If you have a firm faith and belief in God or a higher power, the ideas presented in this book can work with that belief. The Buddha encouraged people to not give up their faith or their religion. He was not creating a new religion, he was teaching a practical method for relieving all suffering. His method is firmly based on ethical living, introspection and service – the hallmarks of the Twelve Step way as well.

One way to reconcile our presentation of how karma is the creator of our life experience and the world around us is to consider God as the creator of the law of karma. If God is the ultimate source of all that is, then God created the natural laws that govern our existence.

God is responsible for the law of gravity, the law of time and the law of cause and effect. It may be possible to transcend these laws and enter the kingdom of heaven, but in the meantime we are prudent to work with them. In general, if we jump off a tall building the law of gravity will produce the result of quite a bit of bodily harm. If we try to walk on water the laws of physics demand that we sink into the waves.

Likewise, the law of karma says that "as we sow, so shall we reap." It serves us to be mindful of what we are doing. If we do an action, the result will come back to us. If we are doing or thinking pleasant things then our life becomes more pleasant. If we are doing unpleasant things then our life becomes one of misery.

Some people come to Twelve Step programs and find faith in God. Other people come and find their belief in God changes or disappears. I hold tightly to any belief that increases my peace and brings me more contentment. I have found that living an ethical life of service brings me the most joy.

APPENDIX 1 - ANCIENT INDIAN SCHOOLS OF BUDDHISM

The Buddha taught for over forty years and each of his presentations were geared to match the audience he was teaching to. Later, his teachings were grouped into four schools of thought. These do not represent actual schools or any modern-day Buddhist sects.

The major differences between each school is its description of correct world view and the definition of the gakja. Each of us will find that we naturally fall into one of these schools of thought based on the view of emptiness we are most comfortable with. This book is based on the Prasangika school ideas which is the view held by the Gelugpa lineage of Tibetan Buddhism. They purport that all existing things are dependent on our calling them and thinking of them as we do.

Gelugpas consider Prasangika the highest view, but others purport that another view, that of the Shentong is more refined. The Shentong school would be included in the chart below as a subset of the Madhyamikas and might be called the *clear light mind school*. They believe ultimate reality has both emptiness and luminosity.

hinayana

Functionalist Schools

1) *Abhidharma School (knowledge school)*

2) *Sautrantika or Sutra School (logic school)*

3) *Chittamatra or Yogachara School (mind only school)*

mahayana

Madhyamika (middle way)

4a) *Svatantrika (independent school)*

4b) *Prasangika (implication or consequence school)*

REFERENCES AND RESOURCES

Alcoholics Anonymous: aa.org
    Big Book of Alcoholics Anonymous

Asian Classics Institute (ACI) free course materials at ACIDharma.org
    Formal Study Courses – Courses 1 to 18
    Daily Practice Course – Courses 1 to 9

Bernadette Roberts: bernadettesfriends.blogspot.com
    The Path to No-Self – Life at the Center
    The Experience of No-Self
    What is Self

Dharma Treasure Buddhist Sangha led by Master Culadasa (John Yates): dharmatreasure.com

Dorena Rode
    Events, classes and blog: TESLI.org
    The Answers are within (ISBN 978-1-941894-00-2)

Ho'oponopono and Dr Hew Len: self-i-dentity-through-hooponopono.com

Master Shantideva
    Guide to the Bodhisattva's Way of Life

Progressive Stages of Meditation on Emptiness by Khenpo Tsultrim Gyamtso Rinpoche. Gives brief descriptions of the various Buddhist schools of thought on emptiness including the Shentong approach.

The Enlightenment & Simple Living Institute
    Retreats, Events, Talks, and blog: TESLI.org

Vipassana Meditation Courses by S.N. Goenka: dhamma.org

Other Books on Twelve Steps and Buddhism
One Breath at a Time - Buddhism and the 12 Steps by Kevin Griffin, 2004
Burning Desire - Dharma God & the Path of Recovery by K.Griffin, 2010
12 Steps on Buddha's Path Bill, Buddha, and We by Laura S., 2006
The 12-Step Buddhist by Darren Littlejohn, 2009
The Zen of Recovery by Mel Ash, Tarcher/Putnam, 1993

ABOUT THE AUTHOR

Dorena Rode (Upasika Mahakhema) joined her first Twelve Step fellowship in 1989 and is currently an active member of multiple programs. She has started groups, led meetings and served at the group level and above. Although not a member of Alcoholics Anonymous she can quote the *Alcoholics Anonymous* "Big Book" with the best of them and is familiar with the literature of the major Twelve Step programs. Because of her unique background she uses the Twelve Step program as an effective way to improve life, not just combat addictions.

After close to twenty years in Twelve Step programs, Dorena began studying with the Asian Classics Institute. The teacher training program she completed was developed by Geshe Michael Roach, the first westerner to earn a Geshe degree (twenty-five years training) at a Tibetan Monastery. He is also the author of the international bestseller, *The Diamond Cutter*. Devoting herself full-time to the training, Dorena completed the eighteen course teacher training program and earned the degree of Maroke (Guide) in 2010. She began teaching Buddhism in the San Francisco Bay Area in 2011 and is currently teaching Asian Classics Institute classes online.

In addition to her study of the classical Tibetan Buddhist texts under Geshe Michael Roach, Dorena subsequently has studied with Master Culadasa, the leader of the Dharma Treasure Sangha whose teachings emphasize nonsectarian Buddhism. She maintains an active internal arts practice. Starting in 1995, Dorena studied Chi Gung and Tai Chi with Richard Upton and more recently Ba Gua and Hsing Yi with Tom Morrissey (student of late Master Kenny Gong).

Dorena's academic and career paths have predominantly been in the field of alternative medicine. It was curiosity about the mysteries of life that led her to study chemistry and receive an undergraduate degree in that field with highest honors in 1988 (UC Santa Cruz). This was accomplished despite having dropped out of high school and running away from home at fifteen years of age. Still searching for answers to how things work (specifically how herbs affect the body) Dorena returned to school (UC Davis) and earned a doctorate in physiology in 2004. Her doctoral research was funded by a personal predoctoral grant from the National Institute of Health – National Center for Complementary and Alternative Medicine.

Dorena is the mother of one grown daughter and currently lives in Phoenix, Arizona where she is active in the Twelve Step community and dedicated to practicing the Steps on the Path to Enlightenment.

THE TWELVE STEPS OF ALCOHOLICS ANONYMOUS

1. We admitted we were powerless over alcohol—that our lives had become unmanageable.

2. Came to believe that a Power greater than ourselves could restore us to sanity.

3. Made a decision to turn our will and our lives over to the care of God as we understood Him.

4. Made a searching and fearless moral inventory of ourselves.

5. Admitted to God, to ourselves, and to another human being the exact nature of our wrongs.

6. Were entirely ready to have God remove all these defects of character.

7. Humbly asked Him to remove our shortcomings.

8. Made a list of all persons we had harmed, and became willing to make amends to them all.

9. Made direct amends to such people wherever possible, except when to do so would injure them or others.

10. Continued to take personal inventory and when we were wrong promptly admitted it.

11. Sought through prayer and meditation to improve our conscious contact with God, as we understood Him, praying only for knowledge of His will for us and the power to carry that out.

12. Having had a spiritual awakening as the result of these Steps, we tried to carry this message to alcoholics, and to practice these principles in all our affairs.

THE TWELVE STEPS AS A PATH TO ENLIGHTENMENT

1. We admitted we were powerless over what we hoped we could control – that our lives had become unmanageable.

2. Came to believe that we could know peace.

3. Made a decision to turn our will and our lives over.

4. Made a searching and fearless moral inventory of ourselves.

5. Admitted to all that is, to ourselves, and to another human being the exact nature of our actions.

6. Were entirely ready to release all obstacles to peace.

7. Humbly dedicated ourselves to the path.

8. Made a list of all persons we had harmed, and became willing to make amends to them all.

9. Made direct amends to such people wherever possible except when to do so would injure them or others.

10. Continued to take personal inventory and when we were wrong promptly admitted it.

11. Sought through prayer and meditation to improve our awareness of ultimate reality and connection to our intuitive center, praying only for knowledge of right action and the power to carry that out.

12. Having had a spiritual awakening as a result of these steps, we tried to carry this message to others and to practice these principles in all areas of our lives.

INDEX

6) We are relieved from the obsession

7) God doesn't remove our shortcomings but we learn how to react differently to them.

8) Enlightenment is something we create / not given to us?

Step Six: It is impossible for mental afflictions or character defects to occupy the same mind at the same time as correct world views

It is truely me ∴ You do not cause my reactions &
- Stop responding from emotions, anger, fear

MY ~~XXXXXXXX~~
Experience / perspective / belief System
   ↓   ↓   ↓
Drug Addict   High Function

How do you feel compassion if you detach